Study Guide for Book Clubs: The Lincoln Highway

KATHRYN COPE

CONTENTS

INTRODUCTION

Few things are more rewarding than getting together with a group of like-minded people and discussing a good book. Book club meetings, at their best, are vibrant, passionate affairs. Each member will bring a different perspective, and ideally, there will be heated debate.

Nevertheless, a surprising number of book club members report that their meetings have been a disappointment. Even when their group enjoyed the book in question, they could think of astonishingly little to say about it and soon wandered off-topic altogether. Failing to find interesting discussion angles is the single most common reason for book group meetings to fall flat. Most groups only meet once a month, and a lacklustre meeting is frustrating for everyone.

Study Guides for Book Clubs were born from a passion for reading groups. Packed with information, they take the hard work out of preparing for a meeting and ensure that your book group discussions never run dry. How you choose to use the guides is entirely up to you. The 'Style', and 'Setting' chapters provide useful context which may be worth sharing with your group early on. The all-important list of discussion questions, which will probably form the core of your meeting, can be found towards this guide's end. To support your responses to the discussion questions, you will find it helpful to refer to the 'Themes & Imagery' and 'Character' sections.

A detailed plot synopsis is provided as an aide-memoire to recap the story's finer points. There is also a quick quiz – a fun way to test your knowledge and bring your discussion to a close. Finally, the guide concludes with a list of further reads similar in style or subject matter.

This guide contains spoilers. Please do not be tempted to read it before you have finished the original novel, as plot surprises will be ruined.

Kathryn Cope, 2022

AMOR TOWLES

Amor Towles was born in 1964 and raised in Boston, USA. After graduating from Yale University, he received an MA in English from Stanford University. His debut novel, *Rules of Civility*, was published in 2011. Set in the 1930s, it tells the story of Katey Kontent, a girl from the Bronx who reinvents herself as a lady of Manhattan high society. Praised for its stylish tone, witty dialogue and vivid evocation of the historical period, *Rules of Civility* marked Towles out as an exciting literary talent, giving him the courage to give up a career in finance to write full-time.

Towles' second novel, *A Gentleman in Moscow* (2016), combined the author's attraction to the historical period of the 1920s and 1930s with his interest in Russian literature and culture. Spanning more than thirty years, it focuses on the experiences of a Russian aristocrat under Stalin's regime. Loved by readers and critics alike, *A Gentleman in Moscow* stayed on the *New York Times* bestseller list for two years.

The much-anticipated *The Lincoln Highway* (2021) debuted at number 1 on the *New York Times* bestseller list. The story recounts the ten-day journey of three teenagers and an eight-year-old boy across 1950s America.

STYLE & GENRE

Structure

Amor Towles is well known for the playful and meticulous construction of his novels. The author sometimes spends years perfecting a book's structure before he moves on to writing it. *The Lincoln Highway* is a prime example of the ingenuity with which he builds his narratives.

Beginning on June 12, 1954, the novel squeezes a great deal of action into ten days. Unconventionally, the chapter numbers are in reverse order, starting with Ten and ending with One. This indicates which day it is in the narrative and acts as a countdown to the novel's conclusion. The technique gives the reader the feeling that all the events are building to one inevitable conclusion. Duchess's death (like that of a tragic Shakespearean hero) is the consequence of everything that has happened up to this point. Ironically, the end of Duchess's life coincides with the true beginning of Emmett and Billy's journey as they return to Times Square to at last begin their route along the Lincoln Highway.

Echoing the reverse countdown of the chapters are other references to countdowns in the novel: Emmett's private countdown from ten whenever he fears losing his temper, the countdown of vaudevillian magic acts, and Duchess's countdown (cut short at eight) as he tries to grab the money from the rowboat.

Emmett and Billy's journey in the novel constantly takes unexpected detours. As a result, they turn back on themselves and end up travelling in the wrong direction. The haphazard nature of their road trip is reflected in the narrative, which is often non-linear, going back in time before it progresses forward again. These narrative detours sometimes take the form of flashbacks or reflect one narrator taking over from another. A character leaves readers on a cliffhanger, and another narrator takes over, describing the same events from their point of view. By halting the progression of the plot in this way, Towles forces the reader to experience some of the frustration Emmett feels when obstacles prevent him from getting on with his planned journey.

Another clever feature of the novel is how the author describes seemingly innocuous events, only to reveal their deeper significance later. An example is Woolly's observation that the wind always picks up around five o'clock at the Adirondacks. The information seems insignificant – until that five o'clock breeze prevents Duchess from paddling to safety in the rowboat. Another example is the scene where Duchess cares for his sleeping friend Woolly by placing his dangling arm back on the bed. He also leaves Woolly a glass of water, knowing his friend always wakes with a dry mouth. Later in the novel, Duchess faces a similar scenario after Woolly's suicide. Woolly has already poured himself a glass of water as he needed it to wash down the fatal medication. However, once again, his hand dangles to the floor. When Duchess gently places his dead friend's hand on his chest, the reader's sense of déjà vu gives the incident an even greater poignancy.

Easter Eggs

Amor Towles fans will know that there are often connections between his novels. The author places these "Easter eggs" in his books for sleuth-like readers to find. In *The Lincoln Highway*, several are related to Woolly and his family. Woolly's uncle, Wallace Wolcott, who died in the Spanish Civil War, appears in Towles' earlier novel *Rules of Civility*. A kind and gentle soul, who takes pleasure in simple things, Wallace has much in common with his nephew. In *Rules of Civility*, we see

Wallace wrapping his inherited officer's watch for Woolly. In *The Lincoln Highway*, Woolly passes this watch on to Billy. Fans of *Rules of Civility* may also recognise the country house in the Adirondacks as a location in Towles' earlier novel. Meanwhile, the date *The Lincoln Highway* ends (June 22, 1954) is the same day that *A Gentleman in Moscow* concludes.

Punctuation

Another style feature of *The Lincoln Highway* is Towles' quirky use of punctuation. As Woolly learns at school, punctuation clarifies meaning, and Towles finds unconventional ways to demonstrate this point. The quotation marks Woolly places around the name of his brother-in-law, "Dennis", are never explained. However, readers instinctively understand that this captures the self-importance of Sarah's husband. Chapter Five also uses punctuation wittily when two successive narratives conclude with a black line. In both cases, the line represents the narrator being knocked unconscious: first Ulysses by Pastor John, and then Pastor John by Ulysses. Alert readers may also have noted that Towles uses an em dash (—) instead of quotation marks to indicate dialogue. The author favours this technique (also used in *Rules of Civility*) as it presents conversation more naturistically, removing the need to write 'he said', 'she replied', etc.

Narration & Tone

Originally, Amor Towles intended *The Lincoln Highway* to be narrated from the perspective of just two characters: Emmett and Duchess. However, as the novel progressed, the author decided that other characters deserved their place in the spotlight. While Emmett and Duchess still dominated the narrative, he also included sections from the point-of-view of Billy, Woolly, Sally, Pastor John, Ulysses and Professor Abacus Abernathe.

The eight narrators of the novel all possess very distinct

voices which differ in tone. To emphasise their conflicting perspectives and the subjectivity of experience, they often describe the same events in different ways. Duchess and Sally speak in a direct, first-person voice, directly addressing the reader and vividly conveying their personality. The other narratives are told from a third-person perspective as if another person observes and narrates that character's experiences.

Genre

The Lincoln Highway is, at its heart, a coming-of-age novel. On the brink of adulthood, Emmett, Duchess, Woolly and Sally are shown rejecting the fates that seem to be laid out for them (either by family or circumstance) and striking out to forge new lives. Although the novel takes place over only ten days, the journey also involves a growth in self-knowledge for the teenage characters.

However, pigeonholing Towles' novel into just one fiction category is too restrictive. *The Lincoln Highway* pays homage to a variety of literary and film genres. It is a road novel, following in the footsteps of Jack Kerouac's cult classic *On the Road*. It is also a quest, with the plot revolving around Emmett and Billy's plan to find their elusive mother. There are nods to the western in Emmett's resemblance to movie star Gary Cooper and the final showdown between Emmett and Duchess. There is also a sinister flavour of southern Gothic in the character of Pastor John: an evil preacher reminiscent of Robert Mitchum's role in the terrifying movie 'The Night of the Hunter.'

Combining a rich blend of tones, from madcap and humorous, to moving and poignant, *The Lincoln Highway* is also influenced by the picaresque. Like Huckleberry Finn following the Mississippi or Dorothy on the yellow brick road, Emmett and co. meet a dazzling cast of colourful characters on their journey, from nuns and panhandlers to circus performers, vaudeville acts and drunken aristocrats.

Some are helpful, while others throw obstacles in their way or have sinister intentions. At times the adventures of the characters are so implausible they seem surreal. Emmett's encounter with Mr Parker and Mr Packer, for example, has the strange, dreamlike quality of Alice coming across the Mad Hatter's tea party in *Alice's Adventures in Wonderland*.

Emmett + Billy are brothers

PLOT SYNOPSIS

Note to readers –

Amor Towles presents the chapters of *The Lincoln Highway* in reverse order, beginning with Ten and ending with One. During the novel, the narrators' perspectives often overlap, meaning the plot summary sometimes goes backwards before it moves forwards again.

TEN (June 12th, 1954)

Emmett

Emmett Watson is driven back to his hometown of Morgen, Nebraska, by Warden Williams. Emmett has been serving a sentence at a work farm for juveniles in Salina since accidentally killing another teenager. Although sentenced to eighteen months, he was released early to care for his eight-year-old brother, Billy. Emmett and Billy's father recently died of cancer.

Emmett is greeted by his neighbour, Ed Ransom. Also waiting for him is the banker, Tom Obermeyer. Obermeyer tells Emmett that his father took out loans to improve the family farm. The bank is now foreclosing on the property, as Mr Watson failed to keep up with the repayments. Consequently, Emmett and his brother must vacate the family home within the next few weeks. Emmett takes the news calmly. However, he tells Obermeyer that he cannot take the Studebaker as he bought the car while working as a carpenter.

Ed Ransom and his daughter Sally have cared for Billy in Emmett's absence. Ed points out that the family of Jimmy Snyder (the seventeen-year-old boy Emmett killed) will be unhappy about Emmett's early release. He suggests that he and his brother should start a new life elsewhere. Emmett confirms this is his intention but refuses to accept a loan from Ed.

Sally Ransom arrives in her old pickup truck, Betty, along with Billy. She is wearing her best dress and has gone to considerable trouble preparing the house for Emmett's return.

Once they are alone, Emmett suggests to Billy that they should move to Texas. He plans to make money by renovating a series of run-down houses. However, Billy is adamant that they should move to California. He takes nine postcards from his backpack and explains that he found them after their father's death. The postcards are from their mother, who left her family on the fifth of July, eight years earlier. Each one was sent from a different destination over nine days.

On a map, Billy shows Emmett the Lincoln Highway: a road traversing America from Times Square, New York City, to Lincoln Park, San Francisco. From the locations of the postcards, Billy has surmised that their mother must have taken this route, ending up in San Francisco. He believes she sent the cards so her sons would follow her to California. Sceptical, Emmett points out how difficult it would be to find her in San Francisco. However, Billy reminds his brother how much their mother loved the Fourth of July firework displays. As her final postcard refers to the fireworks in Lincoln Park, Billy is confident they will find her there.

Emmett checks on his blue Studebaker in the barn. Discovering the battery is dead, he opens the trunk. Inside is an envelope containing a letter, a page from Ralph Waldo Emerson's *Essays* and three thousand dollars. In the letter, Emmett's father apologises for failing to pass on the wealth

14

he inherited from his own father. However, he declares that Emmett will undoubtedly achieve great things with the little he can leave him. As Emmett absorbs his father's last words, he is surprised by the appearance of two visitors: Duchess and Woolly.

Duchess

Duchess and Woolly are fellow inmates from the work farm in Salina. Duchess tells Emmett that they travelled there hidden inside the trunk of the warden's car. Emmett invites his friends to stay for dinner but insists that he will drive them back to Salina in the morning. He reminds them that they only have a few months left to serve their sentences. However, Duchess is adamant that they will not go back to Kansas. He claims that Woolly was desperate to escape.

Duchess asks for Emmett's help. He explains that Woolly's grandfather left his grandson a trust fund of one hundred and fifty thousand dollars, but Woolly's brother-in-law declared him 'temperamentally unfit' to inherit. Fortunately, Woolly's great-grandfather left precisely the same amount of money in a safe at his summer home in the Adirondacks. Duchess claims that if they help Woolly retrieve the money, he will divide it three ways. However, they must do so before the last weekend in June when the family reopens the house. Duchess adds that he also needs to visit his father in New York on the way. Emmett refuses to consider the proposal. He offers to take Duchess and Woolly to the bus station on Monday before he and Billy start their journey.

After dinner, Emmett visits Ed Ransom for assistance with his dead car battery. Meanwhile, Billy tells Duchess and Woolly about the quest for their mother. He describes the house he would build in San Francisco if he had fifty thousand dollars, and Woolly draws a detailed floor plan of Billy's vision. When Woolly and Billy go upstairs, Duchess searches the house for alcohol. He finds a drawer of unpaid bills in Mr Watson's desk.

Woolly stares at the airplanes hanging from Billy's bedroom ceiling, thinking about his father who died in a fighter plane. Billy rereads his favourite book: *Professor Abacus Abernathe's Compendium of Heroes, Adventurers, and Other Intrepid Travelers.* Duchess tells Billy that his name comes from his birthplace (Duchess County) and that his father was a travelling Shakespearean actor. Instead of reading Billy a story, he recounts the violent tale of *Macbeth.*

Duchess privately recalls how his father abandoned him when he was Billy's age. After leaving their expensive hotel without paying, Harry Hewett dropped his son off at an orphanage and drove off with a magician's assistant.

NINE (June 13th, 1954)

Emmett

Emmett wakes up to find Sally cooking breakfast for Billy and Duchess in the kitchen. Duchess praises the homemade preserves, but Emmett tells Sally she should not have gone to so much trouble. Sally is angry after learning from Duchess that Emmett and Billy are planning to leave for California. Emmett insists that he was going to tell her, adding that Sally's father suggested they should make a new start.

Emmett drives into town to buy supplies for the journey. On the way, he pulls over at the fairground site – the location of Jimmy Snyder's death. The accident occurred when Jimmy taunted Emmett, implying that his father was a failure and a coward. Although Emmett tried to ignore the insults, when Jimmy continued, he lost his temper and punched him in the face. Toppling backwards, Jimmy hit his head on a cinderblock, fell into a coma and eventually died. After his death, Jimmy's friends claimed that the assault was unprovoked. Ignoring advice from his attorney, Emmett refused to tell his side of the story in court. Declining a trial, he decided to accept whatever sentence he was given.

In Morgen's library, Emmett compares the population growth statistics of Texas and California. Although he believes Billy's hope of finding their mother is naïve, he decides that California is the best location for house renovations. Noticing the librarian staring at him, Emmett assumes that she recognises him as Jimmy Snyder's killer. However, when Ellie Matthiessen introduces herself, she comments on his resemblance to Billy. Ellie speaks fondly of Emmett's brother, a frequent visitor to the library.

Returning to his Studebaker, Emmett sees three young men standing by the car. He recognises one as Jimmy Snyder's brother, Jake, and another as Eddie Andersen. The third group member is a tall stranger wearing a cowboy hat. Jake looks uncomfortable as the stranger declares his friend has "'unfinished business'" with Emmett. A small crowd gathers. Urged on by the cowboy, Jake hits Emmett, who does not attempt to defend himself. The third punch knocks Emmett to the ground. Sheriff Petersen arrives, and the crowd disperses. Petersen takes Emmett home, where his wife tends to the teenager's injuries.

Duchess

Ignoring Emmett's instructions to lie low at the farmhouse, Duchess hitches a ride into Morgen. Seeing the crowd gathered around Emmett and Jake, he notes how the cowboy stirs up trouble. Duchess watches Emmett admiringly as he takes Jake Snyder's punches. When Sheriff Petersen arrives, the cowboy quickly walks away, and Duchess follows him.

Duchess recalls his time at St. Nicholas's Home for Boys: an orphanage run by nuns. He remembers that Sister Agnes frequently talked about "'the Chains of Wrongdoing'", explaining that every individual will wrong others and have wrong done to them. The result is a heavy burden of guilt and anger that can only be lifted by "'atonement'" and "'forgiveness.'" Duchess interpreted Sister Agnes's advice as similar to completing financial accounts: the key was to balance the harm you inflicted on others against the damage done to you. Duchess realises that Emmett has balanced his moral accounts through his actions. After creating a 'debt' by killing Jimmy Snyder, he repaid it by allowing Jake Snyder to punch him. Duchess feels that this is fair but remains angry at the troublemaking cowboy. Confronting the stranger in an alley, he hits him with a length of wood. As the cowboy lies on the ground, Duchess declares his "'debt repaid in full.'"

Woolly

Billy reads Woolly a summarised version of *The Count of Monte Cristo* from Professor Abernathe's *Compendium*. Afterwards, Billy asks Woolly what Salina was like. Woolly says that every day at Salina was the same. This was also the case at the three boarding schools he attended.

In his second junior year at St. Mark's school, Woolly jumped in a taxi, deciding to visit his sister Sarah in Hastings-Hudson. Although the journey took several hours and cost one hundred and fifty dollars, Sarah paid the fare with no complaint. Brother and sister talked happily until Woolly's brother-in-law "Dennis" arrived home. Dennis was not pleased to see Woolly and even more annoyed to find his dinner unprepared. As his brother-in-law complained about his long working day at the bank, it occurred to Woolly that the dull routines at boarding school were designed to prepare students for the monotony of working life. He tells Billy that he longs for a "'one-of-a-kind kind of day.'"

Sally

Sally is angry after hearing a sermon on the parable of Martha and Mary in church. She refuses to believe that Jesus would criticise Martha for cooking and cleaning instead of sitting at his feet like Mary. Sally feels that her relentless cooking, housekeeping, and preserve making goes unappreciated by both her father and Emmett.

Duchess

When Emmett returns to the farm with facial injuries, Duchess expects him to lie about how he came by them. However, Emmett tells Billy the truth and assures his brother that he counted to ten instead of hitting Jake Snyder back. During the night, Duchess roams around the house when everyone else is asleep. Unaware that Emmett keeps his car keys above the Studebaker's visor, he searches his friend's pockets in vain. A car pulls up outside, and Duchess finds a package left by the door. Recognising his name on it, he looks inside.

EIGHT (June 14th, 1954)

Emmett

Early in the morning, the boys set off in the Studebaker. Duchess declines to map read claiming that he suffers from motion sickness, so Billy takes charge of the navigation. Emmett wants to take the fastest route, but Billy wants to travel the whole journey on the Lincoln Highway. Emmett estimates that it will take four days to reach San Francisco after dropping Duchess and Woolly off at the bus station in Omaha.

Duchess asks if they can make a brief stop in Lewis, Nebraska, as he lived there as a child. Instructing Emmett to pull up at the back of a large building, he declares he will pop in to say hello. When Duchess fails to return after five minutes, Emmett goes to investigate. He finds glass broken in the back door and spoons scattered over the kitchen floor. Hearing a commotion upstairs, he discovers sixty boys eating Sally's strawberry preserves in a dormitory. Emmett realises the building is an orphanage.

Duchess has trapped the nuns in their rooms by jamming chairs under the door handles. Hearing their shouts, Emmett lets them out. Most of the sisters are furious at Duchess, but

Sister Agnes is pleased to hear he has charitably donated Sally's preserves.

Outside, Emmett finds Billy sitting alone on the grass. Duchess, Woolly, and the car have disappeared. Billy explains that Duchess has borrowed the Studebaker to travel to New York. He promised to return the vehicle by the eighteenth of June.

Emmett calls Sally, who shortly arrives at the orphanage. Emmett wants Sally to take care of Billy while he takes a train to New York to find Duchess. Billy, however, refuses to stay behind, pointing out that they can begin their journey on the Lincoln Highway from Times Square. Sally orders Emmett to call her from New York.

Before they leave the orphanage, Sister Agnes gives Billy a St. Christopher pendant. She also tells Emmett how Duchess's father abandoned him at the orphanage. Sister Agnes suggests that Duchess needs a friend to steer him in the right direction. She reminds Emmett of the example of the Good Samaritan.

Duchess

Returning to the Studebaker, Duchess sees it as fate when he realises that Emmett's keys are still in it. Woolly, meanwhile, assumes that Emmett has agreed to loan them the car. Realising that Woolly cannot map read, Duchess asks him to find a station on the radio instead. Ignoring all the stations playing music, Woolly skilfully tunes in to commercials, listening to them with complete concentration. Duchess tells Woolly about Leonello's: an Italian restaurant in East Harlem where his father briefly worked as maître d'. The specialty of the house was a dish called *Fettucine Mio Amore*.

The Studebaker runs out of gas, and Duchess has no money. He decides to steal a case of whiskey from a nearby liquor store and offer it in payment for fuel. In the car's trunk, Duchess finds a jack and handle to break into the store. He also finds a package containing three thousand dollars.

Emmett

The Watson brothers arrive at a freight yard. Emmett explains to his brother that they cannot take a passenger train because all his money is in the Studebaker. Billy is excited at the prospect of an adventure. He tells Emmett that Duchess and Woolly had to stow away in the warden's trunk to escape unjust imprisonment. Emmett warns Billy that Duchess's stories are not always truthful. To illustrate his point, he tells his brother what really happened when Duchess escaped Salina to go to the movies. Accompanied by Emmett's Black bunkmate, Townhouse, Duchess got as far as the river but decided to turn back. Townhouse swam across without him, and, instead of returning the way they came, Duchess walked to the road to hitch a ride. The driver who pulled over was a police officer. When Townhouse returned to Salina later that night, the racist warden, Ackerly, was waiting for him, and he was beaten particularly hard. Billy is sad after hearing this story. He says he feels terrible for Duchess, who was clearly too embarrassed to admit that he could not swim.

Emmett leaves Billy at the passenger terminal, warning his brother not to talk to strangers. He asks some staff members when the freight trains run, but they are unhelpful. Finally, a panhandler advises Emmett to wait for the Sunshine East and tells him the best way to board without being seen.

Emmett returns to Billy, who produces sandwiches from his backpack. Billy explains that a woman called Mrs Simpson bought the sandwiches for him from the coffee shop. He assures Emmett that Mrs Simpson could not be classed as a stranger as she told him many details about her life. The Watson brothers negotiate over how long it is necessary to know a person before they can be called a friend. They settle on three days.

Billy's *Compendium* has a blank chapter entitled 'You'. Emmett suggests that Billy could start writing about his own adventure on the train. However, Billy replies that he wants to start his story '*in medias res*' (in the middle) but does not yet know where the middle is.

Duchess

Woolly has visited many of the great tourist attractions of Europe but has seen very little of America. He is fascinated by the orange and blue Howard Johnson's motels they drive past. When they near Chicago, Duchess suggests booking into a Howard Johnson's for the night. Switching on the TV in their room, Woolly flicks through a series of shows to watch the commercials with the volume turned down. He asks Duchess to describe Leonello's on a Saturday night. Duchess says that when he has his $50,000, he will open an Italian restaurant just like Leonello's.

Duchess decides the perfect location for his restaurant is Los Angeles. However, before he can make this fresh start, he must settle one debt he owes and another two that are owed to him.

Emmett

Emmett and Billy board an empty boxcar. While Billy sleeps, Emmett looks at the postcards from his mother. He remembers that his mother showed signs of depression but seemed at her happiest during their family outings to Seward's Fourth of July fireworks.

SEVEN (June 15th, 1954)

Duchess

Duchess and Woolly have breakfast in the Howard Johnson's restaurant. Woolly is mesmerised by the placemats which show all the Howard Johnson's on a pictorial map of Illinois. Duchess visits the men's room and makes a phone call to

Salina. Affecting an English accent, he claims to be Ackerly's uncle and asks for his address. Returning to the table, Duchess realises that Woolly is missing. The Studebaker has also disappeared from the parking lot.

Woolly

Following the map on his placemat, Woolly drives to Liberty Park, where the Abraham Lincoln statue is located. Although many honking horns follow him, he is oblivious to his dangerous driving. Abandoning the car by a fire hydrant, Woolly finds and admires the statue of Lincoln. He is reminded of his great-grandfather, who loved Abraham Lincoln and insisted that his entire family gather at the Adirondacks house every Fourth of July. Woolly remembers how the youngest child under ten was expected to recite the Gettysburg Address at dinner. When it was Woolly's turn, his sister Sarah had to prompt him, and finally, the whole family repeated it together. Woolly returns to the car to see a police officer is writing him a ticket.

Emmett

When the freight train stops in Iowa, Emmett goes in search of food. Jumping from the top of one boxcar to another, he discovers two apparently empty passenger cars. The boxcars are in chaos from a stag party, with scattered feathers and food everywhere. Inside there is a sleeping man with ketchup stripes painted across his face. Finding an empty pillowcase, Emmett fills it with food. He is about to leave when a man with a slice of ham in his breast pocket gets his attention. Mistaking Emmett for a steward, the man asks him to retrieve the half-empty gin bottle from the floor. Introducing himself as Mr Parker, he tells Emmett he has been trying to work out how to reach the bottle for an hour. He then throws a bread roll to wake the sleeping man, Mr Packer.

Emmett tries to leave with his pillowcase, fearing that the

train will soon start moving again. However, Mr Parker blocks his exit and places a fifty-dollar bill in his pocket. Emmett exits the car and climbs back onto the roof just as the train sets off. Running across the top of the carriages, he jumps to the next boxcar as the train rounds a corner. Landing flat, Emmett hauls himself down to the platform. With the train accelerating fast, he realises he must wait until it slows down before making his way back to Billy.

Pastor John

Entering the boxcar, Pastor John is relieved to see that the only other occupant is a young boy. Billy is reading by flashlight, and Pastor John hopes that he may have some food. Pastor John introduces himself, claiming to be a travelling pastor. The truth is, he has just made a hasty retreat after preaching in Cedar Rapids. Gate-crashing a Christian revival meeting, he planned to seduce a young woman from the choir, but the girl's father intervened.

Hearing the jangling of Billy's silver coin collection from his backpack, Pastor John asks to see what is inside. He reaches for the bag, but Billy holds it firmly to his chest. When they start to tussle, Billy shouts something incomprehensible. Pastor John lifts the boy up and resorts to hitting him, but Billy refuses to let go. A sudden noise stops the preacher from hitting the boy again.

Pastor John turns to see a six-foot-tall African American man has entered the boxcar. Recognising the man as Ulysses, the pastor claims that Billy tried to steal his bag. Ulysses is not fooled and ignores Pastor John's offer to split the silver dollars. Opening the door, he orders Pastor John to get off. The preacher says he will leave by the ladder, but Ulysses guides him towards the door. As Pastor John launches into a prayer, he is sent flying out of the fast-moving train.

Ulysses

Ulysses tells Billy he always travels alone but promises to help him safely off the train when it slows down. Staring at the stranger, Billy asks if he left his wife and son to fight in an overseas war. Unnerved, Ulysses confirms that he did. Billy says he knows how Ulysses came by his name. Dismissing the man's claim that he was named was inspired by Ulysses S. Grant, Billy insists he must have been named for the mythical hero Ulysses. Getting out his *Compendium*, he reads the story aloud. Ulysses weeps, struck by the similarities between his own life and that of the mythical hero.

Ulysses met his wife Macie in 1939 in St. Louis. When World War II began, other men signed up to fight, but Macie (now pregnant) insisted that Ulysses should abstain. However, Ulysses enlisted anyway, despite Macie's threat that she and the baby would be gone when he returned. Fighting in Italy, Ulysses received no correspondence from his wife. On returning to St. Louis in 1945, he discovered that Macie had left two weeks after delivering a baby boy. On hearing this, Ulysses returned to the train station and travelled to Atlanta, then took another in a different direction. He has been travelling this way ever since, never staying anywhere for more than one night.

Ulysses believes there will be no end to his journey, but Billy reassures him that Ulysses returned to his wife and son after ten years. This suggests that Ulysses only has two more years to wait. As the train slows, Billy prepares to make his exit, but Ulysses says he can stay. Emmett enters the boxcar from the roof, and before Ulysses can hit him, Billy introduces his brother.

Duchess

Duchess finds Woolly just as the police officer is about to give him a ticket. Claiming that he works for Woolly's parents, Duchess tells the officer that Woolly is mentally challenged. Back in the Studebaker, Duchess drives to an address in South Bend. Explaining that he is calling on someone he knows, Duchess tells Woolly to stay in the car.

Letting himself into the house, Duchess searches for a suitable weapon in the kitchen. He settles on a heavy cast-iron skillet. Meanwhile, Ackerly (the former warden of Salina and owner of the house) is asleep in his chair. Duchess feels a twinge of conscience when he sees a photograph of Ackerly smiling with his grandsons. Nevertheless, he goes ahead and hits him over the head with the skillet. The sound is so satisfying that Duchess is tempted to hit Ackerly again. However, he realises that according to the balancing of accounts, he would then be in 'debt' to Ackerly.

Emmett

Billy continues to read stories to Ulysses from his *Compendium*. Meanwhile, Emmett tries to work out where he will find Duchess. Remembering that Duchess wanted to visit his father in Manhattan, he struggles to recall the name of Harry Hewett's agent.

SIX (June 16th, 1954)

Duchess

At the Sunshine Hotel, Duchess knocks at the door of Room 42. An elderly gentleman answers, but it is not his father. The man tells Duchess he has occupied the room since Monday, but the former occupant left a black leather case behind. The case contains Harry Hewett's accessories for the role of Othello, including a trick dagger. Duchess realises his father must have left as soon as he received a call from the warden saying he had escaped from Salina.

Duchess books two rooms for the night and bribes the desk clerk for information on his father's whereabouts. He is told that Fitzy FitzWilliams might know. Fitzy is a vaudeville performer and old friend of Harry's.

Emmett

When the freight train arrives in New York, Ulysses takes the Watson brothers to a homeless camp on a disused section of elevated freight track. A Black man called Stew greets Ulysses and cooks for the newcomers. Emmett finally remembers that Harry's agent works in the Statler Building.

Woolly

Woolly buys the previous day's newspapers and reads about a Civil Defence exercise. For ten minutes, the streets of New York were evacuated in a test response to an atomic bomb warning. Woolly is enchanted by the photograph of Times Square, deserted.

Duchess

Duchess settles Woolly in bed, monitors his medicine dosage and leaves the radio tuned to commercials. He then goes alone to the Anchor on West Forty-Fifth Street, Hell's Kitchen. Fitzy is uncomfortable when Duchess approaches him and claims not to have seen Harry for weeks. When Duchess buys him a bottle of whiskey, Fitzy apologises for a police statement he made. Duchess says he will consider them "'even'" if he reveals where his father is.

Sally

Sally is angry to discover that her father has bought Charlie Watson's farm. She accuses him of encouraging Emmett to leave and taking advantage of the family's misfortune. At the house, she finds Sheriff Petersen waiting for her.

Ulysses

Stew is amazed when Ulysses declares they will be sleeping at the camp for more than one night. Ulysses has decided it is worth breaking his usual rule so that Billy can class him as a friend.

FIVE (June 17th, 1954)

Woolly

Duchess and Woolly call in on Woolly's sister Sarah in Hastings-Hudson. When they arrive, there is no one home. Inside the unlocked garage, Woolly shows Duchess the Cadillac convertible he inherited from his father.

Duchess drives off on an errand while Woolly finds the house key under a flowerpot and lets himself in. Ever since his mother remarried and moved to Palm Beach, Woolly has spent the vacations at Sarah's house. He finds that the bedroom he usually sleeps in is being painted, ready for a baby. His belongings are in a cardboard box, including a dictionary his mother gave him. Woolly loved the dictionary as it provided certainty about the meaning of words. However, he hated the thesaurus that came with it, as the numerous alternatives for every word confused him. One day, at St. Mark's boarding school, he used gasoline to set fire to the thesaurus on the football field. Unfortunately, this caused an explosion, setting the goalpost on fire.

When Sarah arrives home, she welcomes Woolly but is concerned about him. She explains that Warden Williams has called and assured her that if Woolly returns to Salina for the final five months of his sentence, his punishment for escaping will be lenient. She tries to encourage her brother to return, but he changes the subject. Woolly reminds Sarah of the family game they used to play at the Adirondacks. The whispered phrase, "'The captains were playing cribbage on their ketches'" ended up as "'The Comptons ate their cabbage in the kitchen.'"

Duchess

Duchess drives to Harlem to find Townhouse: the former
Salina boy to whom he owes a debt. On the way, he tries to
calculate the exact size of his debt. He knows that he owes
Townhouse for the cinema 'escapade'. However, he also feels
that he partially repaid him with 'the Tommy Ladue business.'
Tommy was a racist bunkmate who conspired with a guard to
get Townhouse into trouble. After spotting Tommy and the
guard plant stolen cookies amongst Townhouse's belongings,
Duchess moved the Oreos to Tommy's footlocker. When a
search of the room was made, it was Tommy Ladue who was
accused of theft.

Duchess finds Townhouse sitting on a stoop with a gang
of teenagers around him. Explaining that he wants to settle
his debt, Duchess instructs Townhouse to hit him three
times. After much coaxing, Townhouse eventually co-
operates. Duchess notes that he feels greater satisfaction from
being hit than from assaulting Ackerly. As he leaves, he
throws the keys of the Studebaker to Townhouse's hostile
cousin, Maurice, declaring that the car is now his.

Emmett

Emmett leaves Billy with Ulysses while he goes in search of
Harry Hewett's agent. In the Statler Building, he is rudely
dismissed at the first agency he tries. Taking the advice of a
performer with a parrot, he introduces himself at the next
agency as the son of a rodeo owner looking for a
Shakespearean actor. He is given Harry Hewett's address.

Emmett goes to the Sunshine Hotel and discovers that he
has missed both Harry and Duchess. However, the desk clerk
tells him where to find Fitzy. In the Anchor, Fitzy tells
Emmett that he directed Duchess to the Olympic Hotel in
Syracuse. He adds that Duchess planned to visit an old friend

in Harlem first.

Fitzy tells Emmett that Duchess's mother was a beautiful French singer named Delphine who died tragically young. Devoted to her son, she dressed him in fancy clothes and let his hair grow long. For this reason, Harry sarcastically introduced his son as "'the Duchess of Alba'" or "'the Duchess of Kent'", and the name stuck. Fitzy cries when he recalls Harry's cruelties to Duchess. He begins to explain how Harry's son ended up at Salina.

Ulysses

At the homeless camp, Ulysses tells Billy about his encounter with a twister. Caught in the middle of the countryside in Iowa, he ran across fields towards a church as the tornado approached. Reaching the graveyard, he tripped and fell. Ulysses tells Billy that, at that moment, he realised he had been "'abandoned'" by God and must take charge of his fate. Getting to his feet, he saw a casket inside a grave, not yet covered over. Opening the coffin, Ulysses hauled the body out and climbed inside. The next thing he knew, everything went black.

Pastor John

Although injured when Ulysses threw him from the moving train, Pastor John survived. Determined to take revenge, he boarded the next train to New York.

Pastor John finds the homeless camp on the elevated rail track and sees Ulysses sitting with Billy by the fire. Creeping up on them, he listens to the story about the twister and then knocks Ulysses unconscious with a wooden staff. Billy closes his eyes and calls Emmett's name. When Pastor John grabs him, Billy declares himself "'forsaken.'" He then kicks the pastor on his injured leg and disappears.

After finding a shovel, Pastor John encounters Stew and hits him with it. He then takes Billy's tin of silver dollars out of his rucksack. The pastor is about to leave when someone hits him over the head. Everything goes dark.

Ulysses

Ulysses wakes up, thinking he is back in the coffin. He hears Billy shout, Pastor John's cry of pain and the sound of Stew falling to the ground. Picking up the discarded shovel, Ulysses sneaks up behind Pastor John and hits him over the head with it. Billy appears from beneath a tarp, and Stew approaches, still bleeding from the head. Ulysses asks Stew to look after Billy while he deals with Pastor John. Allowing Billy to believe he is taking the preacher to the police station, he carries the preacher to the river.

Duchess

Duchess returns to Sarah's house, where Woolly's sister tends to his facial injuries. Later that night, he sits drinking Dennis's whiskey in the kitchen when Sarah comes downstairs, unable to sleep. She asks Duchess why he was sent to Salina.

Duchess explains that, when he was sixteen, he lived with his father in Room 42 of the Sunshine Hotel. While Harry and Fitzy sang in the subway for spare change, Duchess visited Marceline Maupassant in Room 49. A formerly famous clown, Marceline was a sensitive man who fell on hard times and became an alcoholic. One morning, Duchess found Marceline's dead body hanging from the ceiling fan of Room 49. When the police arrived, it was noted that Marceline's famous gold watch was missing. A search was conducted, and the watch was found in Duchess's pocket. Duchess realised that his father had stolen the watch and planted it on his son when the police started asking questions. His fate was sealed when Fitzy made a false statement saying that he had seen Duchess stealing from other rooms. In court, Harry told the judge that he could not keep his son under control and agreed that he should be sent to Salina.

After Sarah expresses her sympathy, Duchess takes a brown bottle of medication from her pocket, insisting that it will not help her. He hides the bottle in the spice rack, believing he has performed a good deed.

FOUR (June 18th, 1954)

Woolly

Woolly and Sarah visit FAO Schwarz. The store is Woolly's favourite as their grandma brought them there every Christmas to choose a present before taking them to the Plaza for tea. As they leave, a store worker stops them, reminding Woolly he has forgotten his bear: a giant soft panda for Sarah's baby. Sarah asks Woolly to promise he will return to Salina after his visit. Relieved when he does so, she agrees to have tea at the Plaza.

Duchess

Duchess has arranged to pick Woolly up in the Cadillac and then take him to the circus. Meanwhile, he searches Sarah and Dennis's house and makes himself at home. Drinking Dennis's scotch, he listens to Frank Sinatra and admires the singer's suit and fedora on the album cover. He picks up a baseball bat from Woolly's old bedroom and then surveys the contents of Dennis's closet. Woolly's brother-in-law possesses an array of suits and fedoras, and Duchess decides he will not notice if one outfit goes missing.

Emmett

Emmett locates Townhouse in Harlem. Townhouse confirms that Duchess turned up a day earlier, asking to be punched. Emmett realises there must be a connection between this strange request and his own confrontation with Jake Snyder.

Townhouse says that shortly after the visit, two police

officers came looking for Duchess. He takes Emmett to the 'body shop' run by twin brothers, Paco and Pico Gonzalez. The Gonzalez brothers make a double profit by renting out cars booked in for minor repairs. When Townhouse was sixteen, he rented a Buick Skylark convertible from Paco and Pico for a date with a girl. Unfortunately, the owner of the Skylark spotted Townhouse cruising up and down in his car. Townhouse was arrested but would probably have escaped with a warning if he had revealed how he came by the vehicle. Instead, he said he stole it from the Gonzalez garage and received a twelve-month sentence at Salina.

The Gonzalez twins reveal Emmett's Studebaker hidden under a tarp. Emmett opens the trunk to find the envelope of money is missing. Maurice storms in, insisting that Duchess gave him the car, but Townhouse dismisses his cousin. Townhouse tells Emmett that the police returned to the neighbourhood that morning, asking if anyone had seen two white boys in a blue Studebaker. He suggests that, as Duchess clearly got into trouble while driving the car, the Gonzalez twins should transform the Studebaker with one of their famous paint jobs. Emmett is frustrated by the delay but realises he cannot leave before finding Duchess and the money. He agrees to pick the Studebaker up on Monday. Townhouse tells Emmett that Duchess and Woolly are planning to go to the circus in Red Hook that night.

Sally

Sally waits impatiently for Emmett to call at the agreed time. When he fails to contact her, she looks up a number in the phone book.

Emmett

Emmett and Billy arrive at the circus in Red Hook: a small stadium inside a run-down-looking building. As they watch the Sutter Sisters (two cowgirls performing stunts on horseback), Billy spots Woolly in the audience. When they join him, Woolly says that Duchess is visiting friends backstage. Emmett asks Woolly to take care of Billy while he finds Duchess. As he walks away, the Sutter Sisters shoot each other's clothes off until they are naked.

Backstage, Emmett follows the sound of piano music to a luxurious lounge. Women in various states of undress are draped across couches, and Duchess is playing the piano, dressed in a smart shirt and fedora. Duchess greets Emmett enthusiastically and introduces him as the generous friend who loaned him his car. Furious, Emmett asks to speak to Duchess in private.

Emmett tells Duchess he did not lend him the car. Duchess insists that he only borrowed it and reassures Emmett that his money is safe at Woolly's sister's house. When Emmett says the police are looking for him, Duchess claims that it must be because Woolly parked in front of a fire hydrant and almost received a ticket. He tells Emmett that he exchanged the Studebaker for a Cadillac convertible.

A large woman walks in, who Duchess introduces as Ma Belle. She opens one of the bottles of champagne Duchess has bought for the girls. After having a drink, Duchess tells Emmett to wait in the hallway as he needs a word with Ma Belle and the young woman called Charity before they leave. Emmett is waiting, feeling unsteady when Ma Belle appears and pushes him into a room. He hears the door lock and sees Charity waiting for him on the bed. He tries to head towards the door, but his head spins uncontrollably.

Duchess

Duchess is convinced he has done a good deed by leaving Emmett with Charity. However, he had not planned on having Billy to take care of. They drive across Brooklyn Bridge, and Billy excitedly points out the Empire State Building. Duchess reminds Billy that this is the location of Professor Abernathe's office and suggests they visit him. He aims to teach Billy a harsh life lesson, expecting him to meet with disappointment.

On the fifty-fifth floor of the Empire State Building, Duchess is shocked to find an office with Professor Abacus Abernathe's name on the door. The elderly professor welcomes them inside and is delighted to learn that Billy has read his *Compendium* twenty-five times. When the author asks Billy what brings them to New York, Billy recounts his whole life story. Abacus inscribes his *Compendium* for Billy, noting that the 'You' chapter has not yet been completed. When Billy explains that he wants to "'start *in medias res*'", the professor assures him he has experienced enough adventures to begin and gives Billy a leather journal. Billy tells Abacus about Ulysses and asks if he thinks heroes can 'return' to different eras. Fascinated, Abacus says he is sure this is possible and asks if he could meet Ulysses.

Woolly

At the West Side Elevated, Billy introduces Abacus and Ulysses. Retelling his story, Ulysses explains how meeting Billy has given him hope. Abacus says that his own life has been entirely different. Rarely leaving his Manhattan office, he has lived his life through books. The professor declares faith in the idea that Ulysses will be reunited with his family when ten years are up. However, he warns that the mythical Ulysses had to complete a task before returning home. The Greek hero carried an oar until he reached a place so far from the sea that people would not recognise it. Once someone asked the purpose of the oar, Ulysses had to plant it in the ground. The professor suggests that Ulysses should undertake a similar task, carrying a spike from the railroad instead of an oar.

Billy and Ulysses say a fond farewell to each other. Billy gives Ulysses the St. Christopher pendant, given to him by Sister Agnes. Replaying the day's events in his head, Woolly happily concludes it has been 'a one-of-a-kind kind of day.'

THREE (June 19th, 1954)

Woolly

At Sarah's house, Woolly, Duchess and Billy wait for Emmett's arrival. Duchess shows Billy how to make *Fettucine Mio Amore* while Woolly sorts the spices in Sarah's spice rack into alphabetical order. Reflecting on how many herbs begin with C, he finds a surprise among them. The phone rings, and Woolly answers the call in Dennis's office. Recognising his sister Kaitlin's voice, he hangs up and places the receiver in the drawer of Dennis's desk.

Duchess

Duchess has assured Billy that his brother will be there for dinner at 8 p.m. To distract him from Emmett's absence, he asks Billy to set the table with fine china. Around 6 p.m., Duchess calls Ma Belle to check that Emmett is on his way. He learns that the medicine in Emmett's champagne knocked him out and that he did not know the address of Woolly's sister. Duchess is relieved when, just before eight, Emmett arrives.

Emmett

Emmett wakes at Ma Belle's with a headache. Ma explains that Duchess wanted him to spend the night with Charity as a treat. He dosed Emmett's champagne with Woolly's medicine to act as a relaxant.

Ma and the other women tell Emmett they have known Duchess since he was a boy, as his father was once the ringmaster. Eleven-year-old Duchess worked backstage, taking customers' hats and pouring drinks. Emmett learns that Duchess has taken Billy to Woolly's sister's, but he does not know where she lives. Ma looks up Wallace Wolcott Martin in an out-of-date copy of the *Social Register*. She discovers that Woolly's sister Sarah lives in Hastings-on-Hudson, while his other sister, Kaitlin, lives in New Jersey. Emmett takes the train to the New Jersey address first. He meets Kaitlin Wilcox, who is friendly until he asks if Woolly is there. Angrily, she questions why everyone is asking her this. Emmett goes to Grand Central Station and catches the train to Hastings-on-Hudson. Taking his fourth taxi of the day, he realises he does not have enough money to get any further. He walks the final three miles of his journey.

The convoluted journey gives Emmett time for his anger at Duchess to fade. He recalls his promise to Sister Agnes and the stories of Duchess's childhood told by Fitzy and Ma Belle. It strikes him that, of all his friends at Salina, Duchess was the only one innocent of the crime for which he was convicted. Nevertheless, he feels annoyed when Duchess answers the door and greets him without a hint of remorse. Grasping him by the collar, he pulls back his fist.

Woolly

As Emmett arrives, Woolly tells Billy he wants to show him something. In his old bedroom, he takes out an officer's watch from an old cigar box. Woolly says that it originally belonged to his grandfather in WWI. The watch was then handed down to Woolly's uncle, who died in the Spanish Civil War. Woolly declares that he is now passing it on to Billy. They are interrupted by a noise that sounds like a gunshot.

Duchess

Duchess encourages Emmett to hit him, claiming it will make them both feel better, but Emmett lets go of him. Apologising, Duchess lists everything he is sorry for — from 'borrowing' the Studebaker to leaving him at Ma Belle's. Handing over the envelope of money and a list of 'expenses', Duchess promises to pay Emmett back after the trip to the

Adirondacks. He adds that he also plans to visit his father in Syracuse. They are interrupted by a loud noise from the street.

Sally

When Emmett failed to call her, Sally did some detective work. Claiming to be a distant relation of Woolly's, she told various men of the cloth that she needed to inform the family of the sudden death of her father. Armed with the numbers and addresses of Woolly's mother and sisters, she called Kaitlin first, who became angry when asked if Woolly was staying with her.

Packing a suitcase, Sally drove for a day and a half to get to New York. Arriving at Sarah's house, she is greeted enthusiastically by everyone except Emmett, who asks Sally what she is doing there. Sally points out that he did not call her, so she wanted to ensure they were safe. She adds that she also received a visit from Sheriff Petersen, but her comment is lost as Duchess announces dinner.

Woolly

Duchess serves his friends *Fettucine Mio Amore*, accompanied by Dennis's wine. When Woolly asks him to perform a magic trick, Duchess miraculously removes a cork from the bottom of an empty wine bottle. Once Duchess explains how the trick is done, everyone wants to try it. Woolly fetches more bottles of red wine from Dennis's store and pours them down the sink. Just as Woolly performs the trick, Sarah and Dennis walk in. Horrified, Dennis observes they have drunk four bottles of his vintage wine. Billy and Woolly correct him, clarifying that they poured three of the bottles down the drain. Dennis asks to speak to Woolly in private.

Woolly follows Dennis into his office, where the phone receiver still sits in the drawer. Dennis explains that they cut short their overnight stay in the city when Kaitlin called complaining that several people had questioned her about Woolly's whereabouts. When she called their house, Woolly answered before hanging up. Dennis angrily lectures Woolly about the opportunities he has wasted. He reminds his brother-in-law that he would have gone to prison instead of Salina if his family had not lied about his age and hired an expensive solicitor. Dennis says that Warden Williams is prepared to allow Woolly back to complete the final few months of his sentence. However, Dennis has decided that Woolly must work for a friend at the New York Stock Exchange instead.

Emmett

Ashamed of his behaviour, Emmett washes the dishes once Dennis and Sarah have gone to bed. Sally joins Emmett and dries the dishes. He knows without asking that Sally feels as bad as he does.

TWO (June 20th, 1954)

Duchess

Duchess and Woolly leave Sarah's home early in the morning while everyone else is asleep. Woolly seems depressed but cheers up as they get closer to the Adirondacks. When they reach the house with a lake in front of it, Duchess is taken aback by its grandeur.

Woolly retrieves the key from under a flowerpot, and they enter the house via the mudroom, containing fishing tackle and a gun cabinet. Woolly wants to show his friend the whole house, but Duchess is eager to get his hands on the money first. Woolly takes him to his great-grandfather's study, where the safe is concealed behind a painting of one of Woolly's ancestors. Woolly looks confused when Duchess asks him for the safe's combination.

Emmett

Emmett wakes up to find Woolly and Duchess gone. Dennis has returned to the city, and Sarah is about to paint the baby's room. Emmett offers to paint it for her while Sally takes Billy into town for lunch.

Sarah tells Emmett she is joining Dennis in town, but they are free to stay until the car is ready. She shows him the note Woolly wrote before he left. The letter is full of apologies and assurances that his sister should not worry about him. It ends with, '*The Comptons ate their cabbage in the kitchen!*'

Sarah says that Woolly's troubles began when their father died. While her brother was at his third boarding school, he went into town and saw a fire truck in a parking lot with no sign of any firemen. Assuming that the vehicle had been forgotten, Woolly returned it to the fire station and walked back to school. It turned out that the fire truck had been parked there while the firefighters were in a nearby grocery store. When they received a call to a fire, they found their fire truck gone. By the time Woolly returned it, a stable had burned down along with four horses. That is how Woolly ended up at Salina.

Woolly

While Duchess goes to the store, Woolly tours the house observing his favourite things and reciting his family memories of each room. After writing a note at his great-grandfather's desk, he leaves it between the salt and pepper shakers in the kitchen.

Upstairs, Woolly looks at the family photographs on the wall, including one of his seven-year-old self and his parents in a canoe. He goes to the bedroom he and his cousin used to share and puts the photo on the bureau. Pouring a glass of water, he unpacks his radio, dictionary, cigar box, medicine, and the brown bottle he found in the spice rack. He hears Duchess return in the car and then a loud 'clanging' sound from the study. Lying on the bed, Woolly takes his medicine and all the pink pills from the little brown bottle. In his mind, he relives his perfect 'one-of-a-kind' day.

Abacus

Professor Abernathe is in a wood near Kansas City. His encounter with Billy has had a rejuvenating effect, reminding him of the vibrancy of life itself. His thoughts are interrupted by Ulysses, who tells him that it is time to go. Abacus follows Ulysses up the embankment and into a boxcar.

Billy

Billy is about to start writing the 'You' chapter in his *Compendium*. He tries to decide what point in his life is *'in medias res'*. From his backpack, he takes out a photo of the picnic at the Fourth of July fireworks in 1946. Billy is a baby, and Emmett and his mother are smiling. So far, he has hidden the photograph from Emmett as he knows it will make his brother angry. However, he is sure that Emmett will be pleased to have it once they are reunited with their mother. After much thought, Billy decides to start the story as Emmett is returning home from Salina in the warden's car.

ONE (June 21st, 1954)

Emmett

At nine in the morning, Emmett is at the body shop in Harlem to pick up the Studebaker. He has arranged to meet Billy and Sally later in Times Square.

Townhouse tells Emmet that two detectives have been asking about him. They claimed that a car like Emmett's had been seen near Ackerly's house on the day that someone entered his house and knocked him unconscious. Paco and Pico reveal the Studebaker, now a bright yellow with added horsepower. The twins refuse to accept payment, declaring that they owed Townhouse a favour.

Emmett meets Sally and Billy under the Canadian Club sign at Times Square. Sally tells him that her truck broke down completely just as they arrived. Emmett finds himself thinking about Duchess instead of the journey ahead. He realises that if Ackerly dies from his injuries, he will be a murder suspect.

Emmett asks Sally what Sheriff Petersen said when he visited her. Sally explains that, shortly after Jake Snyder hit him, one of Jake's friends was attacked in an alley and taken to hospital. Petersen had asked Sally if Emmett had any friends visiting at the time. Sally admits that she lied to the sheriff as she was sure that neither Woolly nor Duchess could be involved. Emmett asks Billy if Duchess and Woolly were with him all the time on the day in question. Billy remembers that Duchess went for a walk that lasted as long as it took to read four stories from the *Compendium*.

Emmett begins driving but soon pulls over, insisting they need to find Duchess and Woolly. Pointing to a hand-drawn star on the map, Billy says he knows where to find them.

Sally

Emmett drops Sally and Billy off at a motel. He tells Sally he will take her back home when he returns from the Adirondacks. Sally says she has no intention of going back to Morgen, and Emmett can take her to San Francisco. Emmett assumes that Sally wants to set up home with him and awkwardly tells her that he and Billy need to make a new life on their own. However, Sally indignantly makes it clear that she has no intention of attaching herself to their household.

When Emmett has driven off, Sally knocks on the bathroom door to check on Billy, who is taking a bath. There is no reply. She opens the door to find the window open and Billy gone.

Emmett

Emmett finds the Wolcotts' house with Woolly's car parked outside. He enters the mudroom, noting the checklist for 'Closing the House' on the wall. The first item on the list is 'Remove firing pins.' Emmett shouts Duchess and Woolly, but there is no response.

Emmett goes upstairs and notices a blank space on the wall among the many photographs. He follows the sound of music to one of the bedrooms. Woolly lies dead on one of the beds with his hands crossed over his chest. On the bedside table is a photograph of Woolly and his parents and two empty bottles. Emmett recognises the blue bottle as Woolly's 'medicine', and the brown bottle has Sarah's name on it.

Looking for a telephone, Emmett hears loud clanging downstairs. He finds Duchess in the ransacked study, attacking the safe with an axe. Duchess looks pleased to see Emmett, but his face falls on seeing Emmett's furious expression. Duchess says Woolly's death is tragic, but it was too late to call an ambulance when he found him.

Ignoring Duchess's argument that they should wait, Emmett declares he is calling the police. However, the phone service is dead. Taking hold of Duchess, he insists they are driving to the police station. Duchess protests that Woolly would have wanted them to have the money. He says they can call an ambulance once they have it and then go to California.

Shoving Duchess outside, Emmett repeats that they are going to the police station. He believes Woolly made up the story about the money in the safe to get Duchess to take him there. Suddenly, Billy appears in the doorway and assures Emmett that the safe exists and the money is inside. Taking advantage of Emmett's surprise, Duchess hits him over the head. As Emmett gets to his feet, he sees Duchess push Billy back into the house and shut the door.

Duchess (the previous day)

After Woolly admitted he did not know the safe combination, Duchess tried everything to get it open. Eventually, he decided to go to the general store to buy some tools. Woolly said he would unpack and have a nap.

Duchess returned to the house. Assuming that Woolly was sleeping, he unsuccessfully tried to open the safe for a couple of hours. After searching the office for the combination, he decided to wake Woolly. The moment Duchess saw Woolly, he knew his friend was dead. Noticing that Woolly's fingers were brushing the floor, Duchess rearranged his hands across his chest. Turning off the radio, he thought better of it and switched it on again, thinking Woolly would like the commercials.

Duchess (21ˢᵗ June)

Duchess tries every weapon on the safe with no success. Outside, he notices an overturned rowboat with a large hole in its bow. He then finds an axe in the boathouse. After only a few swings at the safe, Emmett arrives.

Duchess reasons Emmett is so upset because he has never seen a dead body before. As Emmett pushes him outside, insisting that they are going to the police, Duchess feels his friend is not in his right mind. When Billy appears, Duchess seizes his opportunity. Not wanting to hurt Emmett seriously, he discards a large rock in favour of a smaller one before hitting his friend over the head. He grabs Billy and runs inside the house.

Duchess tells Billy they need to work as a team to get the money from the safe. However, Billy closes his eyes, shakes his head and calls Emmett's name. Meanwhile, Emmett is trying to get back in. When Billy stops chanting Emmett's name, Duchess believes he has made a breakthrough. Then Billy opens his eyes, kicks Duchess on the shin and runs away. The sound of breaking glass indicates that Emmett is about to re-enter the house. Duchess goes to the mudroom and throws a croquet ball at the rifle cabinet case.

Billy

When they arrive at the motel, Emmett says he is going to find Woolly and Duchess, and Billy must stay with Sally. Billy takes his backpack into the bathroom, turns on the taps and climbs out the window. While Sally and Emmett are talking, he runs to the Studebaker and climbs in the trunk.

Billy stays in the trunk until he hears Emmett get out and enter the Wolcotts' house. Sneaking inside, he goes into the empty, ransacked study. The safe has four dials, and Billy opens it on his sixth attempt, notes the piles of fifty-dollar bills, and closes it again. Wandering into the kitchen, he notices Woolly's handwriting on an envelope. Billy hears Duchess attacking the safe with an axe and then Emmett coming downstairs. Hiding, he overhears his brother's raised voice and sees Emmett guiding Duchess out of the house.

As Emmett tussles with Duchess outside, Billy fears his brother is in danger of losing his temper. He decides this is the time Emmett needs his help. Opening the door, Billy announces that there is money in the safe. However, as he does so, Duchess hits Emmett with a rock, and his brother falls to the ground. Grabbing Billy, Duchess pushes him back into the house. Duchess's behaviour reminds Billy of his unpleasant experience with Pastor John, and he realises he has been 'forsaken' again. Kicking Duchess with all his strength, Billy runs and hides under the stairs.

Emmett

Locked outside, Emmett smashes the glass door with his belt buckle. He hears glass breaking in the mudroom, and Duchess appears with a rifle. Unintimidated, Emmett repeats that they are going to the police, as Duchess needs to clear up the business of Ackerly and Jake Snyder's friend. Duchess warns Emmett that he will shoot if necessary. Emmett advances but noticing that Billy has appeared, Duchess points the gun at Emmett's brother. Billy reassures Emmett that Duchess cannot fire the weapon because he is secretly illiterate and could not read the mudroom checklist for closing the house. Realising that the gun has no firing pin, Emmett grabs it from Duchess. As Duchess talks away, swearing he would never have shot the gun, Emmett remembers his promise to Billy to count to ten when he gets angry. He does so, and his anger fades away. Emmett then hits Duchess with the rifle butt, knocking him out.

Emmett plans to drag Duchess into the Studebaker and drive him to the police station. He is interrupted by Billy, who shows him Woolly's letter. The envelope contains Woolly's will, which divides his one-hundred-and-fifty-thousand-dollar trust fund equally between Emmett, Billy, and Duchess.

To Emmett's astonishment, his little brother opens the safe. Billy explains that, based on what Woolly told him about his grandfather, he guessed the combination to be the date of the Gettysburg Address. Emmett realises that if he takes Duchess to the police station, there will be an investigation, and Woolly's will might be contested. Billy assures him that Woolly would want them to have their share of the money.

The Watson brothers clear away the evidence of their presence in the house. Emmett drags Duchess outside and tries to decide what to do with him. He rules out the trunk of the Cadillac, fearing that Duchess might be unable to get out. When Duchess appears to be coming round, Emmett punches him again.

Before leaving, Emmett removes the brown bottle from Woolly's bedside and says goodbye to his dead friend. At the last minute, he remembers to remove Duchess's fedora, placing the hat and Duchess's bag in the Cadillac.

In the Studebaker, Emmett suggests they fetch Sally and start their journey. Billy shows him the fastest route to the Lincoln Highway on the map. However, Emmett suggests they go back to Times Square and start from there once the lights are switched on.

Duchess

Duchess comes round to find himself in a rowing boat on the lake. There is no paddle. He sees the Studebaker driving away and shouts to Emmett but the boat tips dangerously.

Duchess assumes the Watson brothers have driven off with all the money. He then notices piles of fifty-dollar notes stacked up in the bow. Wanting to check the exact sum, he moves forward, but the boat tips, and water streams in through a hole. Duchess realises that this is the boat in need of repair, and Emmett placed stones in the stern to keep it afloat.

Despite his predicament, Duchess cannot help but appreciate Emmett's clever plan. He begins paddling with his hands toward shore, but a breeze takes him back to the middle of the lake. He paddles faster, but the wind blows harder, and the fifty-dollar bills begin to blow away. Duchess stops paddling, stands up and edges toward the money. With every step, more water flows into the boat. Deciding that he will have to grab the cash quickly, Duchess counts down from ten. On eight, he loses his balance, hits his face on the bow and falls on top of the money. Water gushes into the boat, the stern rises, and he falls into the lake.

Sinking deeper in the water, Duchess can see the money on the lake's surface above him and the boat's shadow. Then a curtain is pulled back, and he is in a busy street, surrounded by familiar people, all frozen to the spot. Duchess sees Woolly, Billy, Sarah, and Emmett standing by his yellow car. Calling out, he hears a clock striking and realises Marceline's gold watch is in his hand. Duchess takes off his fedora and bows to all his friends.

SETTING

As we would expect from an American road trip novel, *The Lincoln Highway* transports readers to a variety of landscapes and places stretching from rural Nebraska to the landmarks of New York City. On the way, Towles' characters visit an array of establishments, including an orphanage, a circus, a seedy hotel for down-and-outs, and a majestic country home in the Adirondacks. By portraying the best and worst of what America has to offer, the author celebrates the country's rich diversity. While many places are real and recognisable, Towles imbues them with an air of surrealism.

Salina, Kansas

When Emmett and his friends refer to 'Salina', it is shorthand for the juvenile offenders' work farm they attended in Salina, Kansas. Their early days on the farm are traumatic, thanks to the tyrannical warden, Ackerly, who delighted in physical punishment. However, the atmosphere of Salina improved when the well-meaning Warden Williams succeeded Ackerly.

Life at Salina resembles an army 'boot camp'. The boys are woken early by a bugle and become accustomed to a dull and rigid routine. While most boys can bear the monotony, Woolly finds it insufferable. When he and Duchess escape, he privately decides to die rather than return.

Morgen, Nebraska

Emmett has mixed feelings when he returns to his hometown of Morgen. While relieved to be released from Salina and reunited with his brother, the Midwest farming community holds bad memories for him.

The condition of the Watsons' farmhouse is an unwelcome reminder of Charlie Watson's financial improvidence. More neglected than its neighbours, the house suffers from a sagging roof, peeling paint, and windows that are either stuck open or shut. Like many Americans, Emmett's father was inspired by the pioneering spirit and dreamed of farming his own land. However, the reality of battling the weather of the Great Plains was too much for him.

Morgen also reminds Emmett of the crime for which he was sent to Salina. The fairground is the site where he fatally hit Jimmy Snyder, and Jimmy's friends and relatives are unlikely to let him forget it. Everyone knows everybody else's business in this small town, and Emmett cannot escape from the past.

Emmett leaves Morgen without a backward glance when the bank seizes the farmhouse. He is keen to move on and make a fresh start elsewhere. However, as the novel progresses, his aversion to his hometown fades. When Townhouse takes him around Harlem, pointing out significant places from his formative years, Emmett wishes he could do the same in Morgen. By now, he realises that even his worst experiences in his hometown have made him the man he is.

St. Nicholas's Home for Boys, Lewis

The orphanage, run by Sister Agnes, is one of the first unplanned detours of Emmett's journey. The visit to Duchess's previous home gives a Dickensian touch to the novel. It also provides an insight into Duchess's unfortunate childhood.

New York

When they arrive in New York, Emmett, Billy, Woolly and

49

Duchess all view the city differently. Their varying perspectives reflect their personalities and the many faces of New York. Billy's response is a mixture of intellectual curiosity and childlike wonder. He is mesmerised by the iconic skyline and longs to see Times Square illuminated in all its glory. Emmett, meanwhile, barely notices even the most famous tourist attractions. Focussed on tracking down Duchess, he finds the unfamiliar city busier and more confusing than expected. For Woolly, the Manhattan skyline is intimidating, as the towering buildings scream of industry and success. However, accompanied by Billy, he begins to appreciate the sights with similar, child-like wonder.

Streetwise Duchess is entirely at home in New York, particularly in the city's seedy underbelly. As Emmett visits his friend's old haunts in search of him, he learns how some of these places played a poignant role in Duchess's formative years. The locations and the stories attached to them go a long way to explaining Duchess's less admirable traits.

The West Side Elevated

Emmett and Billy's first night in New York is spent with Ulysses at a homeless camp on the 'West Side Elevated': a disused section of train track suspended above the city's streets. Its lofty aspect gives the Elevated a magical atmosphere. It is both part of and separate from the bustling city.

The Sunshine Hotel

The Sunshine Hotel is the go-to establishment for performers who, for one reason or another, are down on their luck. When he was sixteen, Duchess lived in Room 42 with his father. The hotel has an air of despair, intensified by the history of Room 49. This is where Duchess found Marceline Maupassant's dead body hanging from the ceiling fan. When Duchess searches for his father, he finds he has recently vacated the hotel after learning his son had escaped Salina.

The Anchor

While the Sunshine Hotel is the residence of the desperate, The Anchor in Hell's Kitchen is their choice of bar. Despite its name, Emmett notes, 'there wasn't a man you might call seaworthy' in the place. Unsurprisingly, The Anchor is the favourite watering hole of Harry Hewett and his friend Fitzy. Its seedy, down-at-heel atmosphere provides the perfect setting for Fitzy to tell Emmett the sad story of his and Harry's betrayal of Duchess.

The Empire State Building

According to the introduction of Professor Abernathe's *Compendium*, his office is on the fifty-fifth floor of the Empire State Building. In the 1950s, the Empire State was still the tallest building in the world. Its iconic status causes Duchess (and readers) to doubt whether the professor really works from there. However, in an attempt to teach Emmett a lesson, Duchess suggests an impromptu visit, and they find Abernathe precisely where he claimed to be. This experience's slightly surreal nature highlights faith's triumph over cynicism.

Harlem

Harlem is the home of Townhouse and the location of the Gonzalez twins' body work shop. Duchess does himself no favours when he goes there in search of Townhouse, as white strangers tend to stand out.

East Harlem is also the location of Duchess's favourite Italian restaurant, Leonello's. Although the characters do not visit the establishment, Duchess's vivid descriptions bring the restaurant to life. Given Duchess's tendency to exaggerate, readers sense that the reality may not quite match his enthusiastic accounts.

The Circus, Red Hook

When Duchess books tickets for the circus, it seems an uncharacteristically wholesome activity for him to choose. However, the circus at Red Hook is far from traditional. It is located in the run-down area of Red Hook, Brooklyn, and is comprised of a small stadium inside an unpromising-looking building. The acts, meanwhile, are entirely made up of women: a ringmaster wearing a false moustache, a large woman pursued by seals on a child's tricycle, and the risqué Sutter Sisters who shoot each other's clothes off. This is a 'bawdy' circus, where the performances are surreal and transgressive.

Readers could be forgiven for mistaking the female-dominated circus as a feminist reworking of a traditional entertainment form. However, backstage, Emmett is shocked to find scantily clad women draped across couches, waiting for clients. Duchess is entirely at home here, playing the piano with half-naked women clustered around him. This is because his father was once the ringmaster while eleven-year-old Duchess worked backstage, taking customers' hats and pouring drinks.

The Adirondacks

The Adirondacks provide a startling contrast to the urban setting of New York. The summer home of Woolly's wealthy great-grandfather, this elegant residence screams of old money. Set in the stunning countryside of upstate New York, the huge house overlooks its own lake.

Woolly and Duchess ostensibly go to the Adirondacks to collect the 150,000 dollars from the safe. However, in reality, their goals are quite different. For Woolly, the house represents a longed-for past. Going there is the closest Woolly can get to turning back time and returning to his happier childhood days. For this reason, he chooses to die there.

After Woolly's suicide, the house becomes the location of the final showdown between Emmett and Duchess. As Emmett shows he is determined to call the police, the conflicting motivations of the two friends come to a head. The country pile also becomes Duchess's final resting place when he drowns in the lake.

CHARACTERS

Emmett Watson

Emmett is the eighteen-year-old protagonist of *The Lincoln Highway*. A Gary Cooper look-alike, he also resembles the actor in his character: quiet but with a confident aura of inner strength. The novel begins when he is released early from a work farm for juvenile offenders after his father's death. Principled and mature for his years, Emmett is an unlikely criminal. Although guilty of killing another teenager, he is also the victim of unfortunate circumstances. Provoked, he threw a single punch which turned out to be fatal for Jimmy Snyder when he hit his head on a cinderblock.

On briefly returning to his hometown of Morgen, Emmett faces more misfortune. Greeted by a bank representative, he is told of the foreclosure on his father's farm. He is also confronted by Jimmy Snyder's brother and willingly takes a beating from him. Emmett's lack of retaliation stems from his belief that he has not fully atoned for Jimmy Snyder's death.

Emmett's decisions about his future are based on the life lessons he has learned from his father's failures of judgement. Having seen Charlie Watson battle unsuccessfully with failed crops and unpredictable weather, he chooses carpentry over farming. Deciding where to relocate, he follows his head rather than his heart, researching the most promising places to renovate properties. Emmett also refuses financial assistance, making it clear to Ed Ransom that the Watson family's debts ended with his father.

Emmett embarks on a literal and metaphorical journey in *The Lincoln Highway* as he leaves Morgen to make a fresh start with his little brother. Like a mythical hero, he undergoes trials, and his character develops accordingly. At the beginning of the journey, Emmett's practical streak borders on the prosaic. He is so single-minded that the small pleasures of life elude him. While Billy is keen to take in the sights along the Lincoln Highway, Emmett views this as a diversion from their mission. The thrill of glimpsing iconic landmarks is lost on him, as is the lurid fun of the circus and the seductive qualities of young women. Emotionally repressed, he is almost prissy.

Self-reliance is another of Emmett's virtues which, taken to the extreme, becomes a flaw. While his determination not to be 'beholden' to others is admirable, it is also isolating and sometimes hurtful. Fearing Sally's 'expectations', Emmett often appears gruffly ungrateful for her generosity. At the beginning of the novel, he only has room in his heart for his younger brother, Billy. Responsibility for the welfare of anyone else feels like a burden and a distraction to his purpose. Meanwhile, Emmett's most obvious weakness as a character is his temper. This is the fatal flaw that led him to kill Jimmy Snyder accidentally. In a bid to overcome this failing, Emmett promises Billy that he will count to ten if he has the urge to hit someone.

By encountering obstacles and distractions throughout his journey, Emmett is forced to confront his weaknesses and becomes a more rounded character. His temper is tested to the limit by Duchess, who perpetually places hurdles in the way of his desired destination. Like it or not, Emmett is also forced to ask for Sally's help when Duchess leaves him without transport.

By the novel's end, we see how Emmett has changed as he prepares to hit the Lincoln Highway. Instead of taking the fastest route, he suggests they pick up Sally and start from Times Square once the lights are switched on. The suggestion illustrates that Emmett can now embrace the wonders that the journey may bring, as well as the final destination. However, the hopeful scenario is significantly undercut by the death of Duchess. Oblivious to the ramifications of his actions, Emmett has no idea that, once again, he has accidentally killed someone.

Billy Watson

Eight-year-old Billy serves as a contrast to his older brother. Although he shares Emmett's strong moral code, Billy is open and innocent, anticipating nothing but good from the universe and human nature.

Billy's tendency to see the best in people means he makes friends quickly. Other characters find his unjaded hopefulness infectious. Despite Emmett's doubts about finding their mother, Billy persuades him that they should move to California. After just a short acquaintance, he also inspires Ulysses and Professor Abernathe to take their lives in new directions. Even characters who take a dislike to Billy recognise his innate goodness. Both Pastor John and Duchess find his virtuousness baffling and slightly unnerving.

Intellectually precocious, Billy reads and rereads *Professor Abacus Abernathe's Compendium of Heroes, Adventurers, and Other Intrepid Travelers*. His repetitive routines and adherence to rigid rules suggest Emmett's brother may be on the autistic spectrum. However, there are also times when Billy shows himself to be surprisingly adventurous. A prime example of this combination of qualities is when he climbs out of the motel's bathroom window but first double-checks that the bath will not overflow in his absence.

Billy's taste for adventure is fuelled by his reading matter. Learning about the great heroes (both real and fictional), he concludes that dramatic actions are sometimes a moral necessity. For this reason, he is never without his US Army backpack equipped with a flashlight and compass. Billy also refuses to participate in his school's 'Duck-and-Cover' drill, due to Professor Abernathe's assertion that a hero confronts danger rather than hiding from it.

An important lesson in Billy's journey is that blind faith in

God or other people is sometimes not enough. Ulysses teaches him that, at times of great jeopardy, an individual must rely on his own instincts and resources. Billy puts this advice to good use with Pastor John and Duchess when they have him in their clutches. After calling for his brother proves useless, he saves himself with an ability to deliver a surprisingly hard kick. By the end of the novel, Billy takes on a heroic role, using his intelligence to save the day. His realisation that Duchess cannot read brings a potential armed conflict to an end, while his close attention to Woolly's stories provides the clue to open the Wolcotts' safe.

Duchess

Emmett and Duchess are complete opposites. While Emmett has integrity, he can be strait-laced, overly reserved and a little puritanical. On the other hand, Duchess has a problematic concept of right and wrong but is funny, ·charismatic and a born raconteur. He is also the 'instigator' of many problems, leading to countless diversions in Emmett's journey.

Although Emmett is the protagonist of *The Lincoln Highway*, Towles gives Duchess the advantage of a first-person narrative. Duchess builds a relationship with his audience by confiding in the reader directly, with asides such as 'Now, before I tell you what happened next …'. His narrative fizzes with energy, wit, and irony. Although readers may approve most of principled Emmett, it is hard not to be won over by Duchess's entertaining take on the world.

While Emmett aims to achieve his goals through reason and hard work, Duchess is a reckless grifter who lives for the moment. As the novel progresses, it becomes clear that Duchess's character has been shaped by his upbringing. Travelling with his father – a theatrical con-artist – the main lesson Duchess learned was how to evade moral and financial responsibility. He also experienced betrayal early on when his only surviving parent abandoned him at an orphanage. As we learn more about Duchess's backstory, readers are more and more inclined to care about him. The discovery that he was sent to Salina for a crime his father committed is particularly poignant. Ironically, this makes Duchess the only one among the Salina friends to be innocent of the crime he was accused of.

Duchess's moral compass is shown to be faulty rather than completely absent. Readers follow his train of thought as he convinces himself he is doing the right thing in the most dubious of circumstances. When he attacks Jake Snyder's friend with a length of wood from a dumpster, he thinks of it as 'the work of the Lord' and, consequently, feels 'a welling sense of moral satisfaction'. His confused code of ethics is the result of conflicting influences. While his father taught him how to lie and cheat, his friendship with Emmett introduces him to honour and integrity. Duchess is particularly impressed by his friend's innate sense of fairness when he willingly allows Jimmy Snyder's brother to punch him. Unfortunately, Duchess translates the incident into a literal-minded code based on debt and repayment. He atones for getting Townhouse into trouble by encouraging his friend to hit him three times. However, he also repays Warden Ackerly for his cruelty by hospitalising him with an iron skillet. In Duchess's mind, both acts are equally valid.

Towles shows glimpses of the respectable citizen Duchess could become. His dream of owning an Italian restaurant seems credible when he displays his talents as a chef to his friends. Significantly, he is the only male character who really appreciates the meticulous nature of Sally's housekeeping. There are also moments when Duchess shows himself as capable of genuine kindness. His distribution of Sally's preserves is a thoughtful gesture (despite breaking into the orphanage to do so). Meanwhile, his friendship with Woolly reveals a sensitive, caring side. More than anyone else, Duchess understands and indulges Woolly's quirks, never making him feel inadequate. At bedtime, he behaves like a loving parent to his fragile friend, monitoring his 'medicine', pouring him a glass of water, and tuning the radio to something Woolly will find soothing.

Despite his likeability, there are also moments when Duchess's behaviour is hard to excuse. He shows his selfish streak when he 'borrows' Emmett's car without permission. A petty thief, he has no respect for the property of others, searching friends' houses whenever he is left alone. Duchess can also be mean-spirited, as demonstrated when he suggests calling in on Professor Abernathe. The purpose of the visit is to disappoint Billy, who he considers 'something of a know-it-all'. Although his plan does not have the intended consequences, Duchess's deliberate decision to spoil a young boy's dreams seems particularly spiteful.

Perhaps most shocking is Duchess's demeanour after Woolly's suicide. When Emmett comes across him attacking the Wolcotts' safe with an axe, Duchess seems to have forgotten his dead friend, even greeting Emmett with a smile. However, even this incident is more complex than it first appears. Readers are forced to reassess Duchess's reactions when he gives his account of finding Woolly's body. Knowing there is nothing more he can do for his friend, Duchess tenderly places Woolly's dangling arm across his chest. He also tunes the radio to a station he knows his friend would like. Readers are reminded that this is not the first dead friend Duchess has had the misfortune to find (the first being Marceline Maupassant). This partly accounts for his ability to carry on with the plan to open the safe, regardless. Duchess's recital of the line from *King Lear*, "'The wonder is he hath endured so long'" demonstrates that he is not completely surprised by Woolly's suicide. He always knew his friend was not cut out to cope with everyday life.

Duchess conceals his weaknesses with bravado. Claiming "'[s]mall print gives me a headache'", he covers up his illiteracy — a ruse that works on most of the characters thanks to his ability to quote Shakespeare from memory. Duchess also tries to hide his inability to swim, preferring people to believe that he abandoned Townhouse on a whim during their excursion to the cinema. Only Billy is astute enough to recognise the shortcomings Duchess is so ashamed of. When Duchess threatens him with a gun, Billy confidently asserts that Duchess cannot read, just as he cannot swim. This means he could not read that all firing pins were removed whenever the country house stood empty. Giving up the gun, Duchess immediately swears he would never have shot Billy or Emmett. Readers are left to ponder whether this is really the case.

For Duchess, *The Lincoln Highway* is a not-quite-coming-of-age story. We see him striving to be a better person, but his potential is never fulfilled. Like a tragic Shakespearean hero or the mythical Achilles, he is eventually killed by his weaknesses. His inability to swim plays a part in his death. However, Duchess's greed ultimately proves to be his fatal flaw. Seeing his money blowing away from the rowboat, he cannot help but try to grab it, despite the danger.

Woolly Wolcott Martin

Another former Salina inmate, Woolly originates from a completely contrasting background to Emmett and Duchess. His family are wealthy with their own country estate, and Woolly's ancestors rubbed shoulders with presidents.

The family's money comes from a paper company established by Woolly's great-grandfather. However, despite their wealth, the Wolcott men have proved to be an unlucky bunch. Woolly's grandfather passed away at twenty-five, his Uncle Wallace at thirty, and his father died young in a fighter plane. Sadly, twenty-year-old Woolly seems to attract similar misfortune. Traumatised by the loss of his father, he struggles to accept his mother's remarriage and relocation to Palm Beach. Woolly has also been effectively disinherited by his unpleasant brother-in-law, Dennis. At eighteen, he should have been entitled to the one hundred and fifty thousand dollars his grandfather left him in a trust fund. Dennis, however, has Woolly declared 'temperamentally unfit' to inherit. The absence of his parents and the hostility of his sister's husband make Woolly feel that he does not fit in anywhere.

Woolly is kind and gentle, but his eccentric character gets him into trouble. Before escaping Salina, he was expelled from several of the best boarding schools in the country. Woolly finds the routine of these institutions stultifying, causing every day to feel like 'an every-day day.' He is also incapable of conforming to the 'norms' expected of him. This is reflected in his dislike of rhetorical questions such as, '*When are you going to grow up?*' and '*What in God's name were you thinking!*'

Woolly is never intentionally disruptive, but his whims often have disastrous consequences. At St. Mark's School, his frustration with a thesaurus accidentally leads him to set a goalpost on fire. Meanwhile, his decision to drive a 'forgotten' fire truck to the station leads to the death of several horses and his term at Salina. Woolly's sense that he is constantly at odds with society's expectations gives him 'the blues'. He tries to manage his anxiety and depression with self-prescribed 'medicine', which may be laudanum.

Woolly's struggles in navigating life stem from his unworldliness. He and eight-year-old Billy form a strong bond because they share a similarly innocent perspective on the world. His most endearing quality is his capacity to be amazed by the ordinary. Although he has seen many of the great sights of Europe, Woolly examines a standard hotel room 'like a private detective from another planet.' He is similarly fascinated by the illustrated maps on the placemats in Howard Johnson's.

While Woolly's mind is childlike, he exhibits surprising skills in some areas, applying himself intently to certain tasks. This is demonstrated when he draws an intricate floor plan based on Billy's description of his fantasy home. He is also adept at tuning in a radio, skipping the music to listen to the commercials that he finds so soothing. Woolly loves how commercials present a problem (e.g., grass-stained clothes or lumpy mashed potatoes) and then miraculously offer a solution. They give him hope that all of life's problems might be solved in a similar way.

Despite his frustration with the thesaurus, Woolly is perceptive about language and its use. He has developed his own quirky way of expressing himself, using 'Woollyisms' such as "'absotively'" and "'on porpoise'". He also notices patterns in language that most people overlook, including the fact that most questions begin with the letter W. This insightfulness equally applies to interpreting the tone of voice used by other characters. For example, when Duchess tries to teach Billy a lesson by suggesting they call on Professor Abernathe, Woolly recognises the tone 'that preceded the dispelling of an illusion.' Woolly has heard the same tone many times from his teachers and brother-in-law. Meanwhile, his habit of placing quotation marks around the name "Dennis" conveys the pompous way his brother-in-law introduces himself.

Woolly longs to live in a carefree world, free of routine and the pressure of adult responsibilities. For this reason, he is nostalgic about his childhood and likes to reminisce with his sister Sarah, particularly about the times before their father died. A favourite memory is of their mother declaring, *"'The Comptons ate their cabbage in the kitchen'"* at the end of a game of Chinese whispers. Cherishing these memories, Woolly strives but fails to recapture the past.

Toward the novel's end, Woolly experiences a 'one-of-a-kind kind of day.' After a nostalgic trip to FAO Schwartz and the Plaza with Sarah, he visits the iconic landmarks of New York with his friends. Faced with the prospect of yet another rigid routine (working on the New York Stock Exchange), Woolly decides to quit while he is ahead. Returning to the site of his happiest family memories in the Adirondacks, he quietly takes his own life.

Sally Ransom

Sally is the Watson family's neighbour in Morgen. Her

mother is dead, and her sister has married and moved away. This leaves Sally with the thankless task of keeping house for her father. She also takes on responsibility for Billy's care while Emmett is in Salina.

When Emmett returns from the work farm, Sally makes sure that the Watson house is spotless, the fridge is stocked, and there is a casserole ready to warm in the oven. She also wears her best dress, suggesting a romantic interest in Billy's brother. However, if Sally expects effusive gratitude from Emmett, she is disappointed. Determined not to encourage any womanly 'expectations', Emmett appears almost as ungrateful for Sally's hard work as her father.

Sally is one of only two characters given a first-person narration in the novel (the other one being Duchess). As the only main female character, Towles wants her voice to make an impression. A firm believer in '[p]lain speaking and common sense', Sally is brisk and forthright. In her narrative, she expresses anger and resentment, demonstrating that she is far from the contented little homemaker. A devout Christian, she nevertheless becomes furious on hearing a sermon about Martha and Mary. The praise Mary receives for sitting at Christ's feet while Martha's contribution in the kitchen is ignored seems to sum up the way her own domestic work is undervalued and taken for granted. Sally blames the male gospel writer, who clearly believed that women 'have plenty of time for sitting and listening because a meal is something that makes itself.'

Sally goes above and beyond her domestic duties, baking cookies and going through the painstaking process of preserve making. At the same time, she longs for something more. She hopes, in vain, that her father will remarry so that his care will become another woman's responsibility. Sally's desire for freedom and adventure is reflected in how she drives her old pickup truck, Betty. A fast and erratic driver, she enjoys being alone on the open road. In her narrative, she takes issue with the gendered roles of adventurers in stories, complaining that they are always about 'some man going somewhere.' Sally points out that 'the will to move' is a human rather than a masculine urge, but women are often deprived of fulfilling it.

After rescuing Emmett in New York, Sally is furious when Emmett suggests that he should take her back to Morgen as soon as possible. She makes it clear that she has no intention of returning to her life in Morgen and insists on accompanying the Watson brothers to San Francisco. When Emmett assumes she wants to set up home with them, Sally insists that her days of cooking and cleaning for men are over, and she intends to live alone. Readers are left uncertain whether Sally protests too much in this scene. Certainly, she is attracted to Emmett and loves Billy like a mother. Sally and Emmett are so similar in their moral values and plain-speaking ways that it is easy to foresee them uniting as a family.

Charlie Watson

The death of Emmett and Billy's father takes place before the novel begins. Charlie Watson's passing allows Emmett to leave Salina before his sentence is complete to take care of his younger brother. Unfortunately, he leaves his sons with very little else. The bank repossesses the Watsons' farm to make good on his many loans.

When Duchess searches Charlie's desk, he looks for signs of the vice that led to the loss of the Watsons' farm (empty bottles of alcohol, betting slips, etc.) However, all he finds are piles of unpaid bills in the drawer. Charlie's weakness was not drinking, gambling, or women. Instead, it was an inability to judge when to give up on his American dream.

Originally from an affluent Boston family, Charlie Watson dreamed of a simpler life. Leaving the trappings of wealth behind, he moved to Nebraska to farm his own land. Although unsuited to farming, he persisted in his dream, even after twenty years of failed crops and his wife's departure.

While Charlie was a bad farmer, he tried to be a good

father. Kind and gentle, he gave Emmett his blessing to become a carpenter instead of following in his footsteps. Knowing he was dying, Charlie put aside three thousand dollars for Emmett and a page torn from Ralph Waldo Emerson's *Essays*. In an accompanying letter, he expressed his confidence that Emmett would pursue his own path and fulfil his promise.

Mrs Watson

Emmett and Billy's mother does not appear in the novel, having abandoned her family eight years earlier. However, it is her absence that drives the action of the story. After finding postcards from her (concealed by their father), Billy is convinced they will find their mother at the Fourth of July fireworks in Lincoln Park.

Readers can only guess why Mrs Watson left her husband and sons without warning. Emmett's memories of his mother's distant gaze and distracted air suggest she was deeply unhappy. Rural isolation, financial pressures and post-natal depression could have been contributing factors. In addition, there is the sense that, like Woolly, she yearned to return to the past.

Just like her husband, Mrs Watson was from a wealthy Boston family. Her love of fireworks stemmed from memories of the fireworks she saw at Cape Cod as a girl. When Charlie Watson took her to the Fourth of July display at Seward, he attempted to revive his wife's happiness. However, the event only convinced her that contentment could only be found elsewhere.

Ed Ransom

Ed Ransom is a successful rancher, the Watsons' neighbour, and Sally's father. When Emmett is released, he offers him money to start a new life elsewhere. While Ed claims only good intentions, Sally furiously interprets this as a ruse to keep her away from Emmett. She assumes her father does not want to lose his free housekeeper or disapproves of his daughter mixing with a felon. Ed certainly benefits from Sally's housekeeping skills, but he finds her spirited manner challenging. When he snaps up the Watsons' farm as soon as it goes up for sale, it seems this may be his reason for wanting Emmett many miles away.

Jimmy Snyder

Jimmy Snyder is the seventeen-year-old Emmett accidentally killed. A known troublemaker, he taunted Emmett, insulting his father, until Emmett lost his temper and punched him in the face. Falling backwards, Jimmy hit his head on a cinderblock and fell into a coma.

Jake Snyder

Jimmy's brother, Jake, is presented as a victim of circumstances, just like Emmett. When Emmett returns to Morgen, he feels duty-bound to hit him, even though he clearly does not want to.

The Tall Cowboy

The Tall Cowboy is the nameless instigator of Jake's assault on Emmett, egging him on until he feels he has no choice. Witnessing the event, Duchess recognises the cowboy as the type who stirs up conflict while avoiding danger himself. Confronting the troublemaker in an isolated alley, Duchess teaches him a lesson with a length of wood, leaving him unconscious.

Harry Hewett

Harrison Hewett is a travelling variety performer who specialises in Shakespearean monologues. Duchess succinctly describes his father as having 'the nose, chin, and appetites of John Barrymore.' For those unfamiliar with the 1920s film star, Barrymore was famous for his aristocratic profile and his predilection for alcohol and women.

Harry's real talent is as a con man and escape artist. Exploiting his refined accent and respectable bearing, he often rang up huge bills at expensive hotels before exiting via the fire escapes. When Duchess was eight, he extended his vanishing repertoire by abandoning his unsuspecting son at an orphanage before driving away with a glamorous magician's assistant.

Harry's dissembling nature is symbolised in the black leather case containing his accessories for the role of Othello. Duchess reveals that the black face paint came in handy on stage and when his father disguised himself to avoid paying bills. Meanwhile, the dagger, like Harry, is a fake. The blade is designed to retract when Othello stabs himself, and the 'jewels' on the handle are made of paste. However, Duchess initially believes Harry's claim that a 'master craftsman' forged the blade. He discovers this is just another of his father's lies when he tries to prise a safe open with the dagger, and the blade snaps.

The true depth of Harry's heartlessness is revealed when we learn that he stole a watch from Marceline Maupassant's dead body and framed Duchess for the crime. Instead of begging for leniency on behalf of his son, Harry did his best to ensure that Duchess served a custodial sentence. Feigning sorrow in court, he even took the opportunity to recite a speech from *Hamlet*.

Harry remains elusive in the novel despite his son's attempts to find him and settle old scores. Duchess discovers that, as soon as his father learned he had absconded from Salina, he made a characteristically speedy exit from the Sunshine Hotel. He traces Harry to the Olympic Hotel in Syracuse but, as far as readers know, does not get the chance to visit him. Nevertheless, it is possible that Duchess chooses to omit this encounter from his narrative.

Delphine

Duchess's mother, Delphine, died when her son was young. A beautiful French singer, she was as devoted to Duchess as Harry was indifferent. Her habit of dressing him in fine clothes and letting his hair grow long led to his unofficial renaming from Daniel to Duchess. At the sight of his son dressed like a prince, Harry would sarcastically introduce him as "'the Duchess of Alba'" or "'the Duchess of Kent'". Readers can only imagine Duchess's feelings after his loving mother's death when he was left in the 'care' of his callous father.

Fitzy FitzWilliams

Fitzy is an old friend of Harry Hewett. When he encounters the washed-up performer, Emmett learns that Fitzy helped Harry to frame Duchess for the theft of Marceline's watch. He added credibility to his friend's story by claiming he had seen Duchess steal from other hotel rooms. Unlike Harry, Fitzy feels remorse for his role in Duchess's downfall.

During his theatrical career, Fitzy made the most of his long, white beard. He progressed from reciting poetry as a Walt Whitman impersonator to playing Santa Claus at Christmas parties held by the rich. Hired at extortionate fees during December, he became so wealthy there was no need to work for the rest of the year. However, his unfortunate agreement to a gig playing Karl Marx ruined his career. Condemned as a Communist 'provocateur', he became a 'third-rate' vaudeville performer, reciting poetry during the intervals. By the time Emmett meets him, he has drunk away all the money he ever made. Living in the Sunshine Hotel, he survives by reciting lewd limericks on the subway.

Pastor John

Pastor John introduces a sinister flavour of southern Gothic into *The Lincoln Highway*. The self-proclaimed preacher travels the country using his religious credentials to prey on the vulnerable. He thinks he has hit the jackpot when he finds himself alone with Billy and a collection of silver dollars inside a boxcar. However, Billy is surprisingly resistant to his wheedling and the preacher resorts to hitting the eight-year-old boy. Divine justice eventually intervenes when Ulysses throws Pastor John off the train. Ironically, throughout the encounter, Billy shows himself to be the better Christian, even expressing concern about the preacher once Ulysses has ejected him. The incident acts as a lesson to Billy that not all strangers are well-intentioned.

Pastor John is ideally suited to preaching as he likes nothing better than the sound of his own voice. He delights in biblical language, particularly when equating his loathsome behaviour to 'the vengeance of the Lord' and 'God's will.' However, his knowledge of certain parts of scripture is shown to be sketchy. For example, when he claims that light was "'The Lord's first creation'", Billy correctly points out that God made heaven and earth first. In his narration, the preacher also confesses to a distinctly ungodly habit of purchasing 'female companionship.'

Later on in the novel, Pastor John reappears when he viciously assaults Ulysses and again tries to steal Billy's silver dollars. This time Ulysses knocks him unconscious and carries him to the river to dispose of. Readers are left uncertain if this is the end of the odious Pastor John.

Ulysses Dixon

When Billy first sees Ulysses, it is as if an archetypal hero has just stepped out of the pages of his *Compendium*. The six-foot-tall African American man first appears when Billy is in need of rescue from the clutches of Pastor John in a boxcar. On learning his name, Billy is certain that the imposing Black man was "'named for the *Great* Ulysses'" and not Ulysses S Grant, the former president and leader of the Union army.

Questioning Ulysses, Billy uncovers several similarities between him and the mythical hero. Both reluctantly left their wife and son to fight in an overseas conflict (the Trojan War and World War II). Both also met with obstacles when trying to return to their families. While the Great Ulysses' ship was blown off course, Towles' Ulysses returned to St. Louis to find that his wife had fulfilled her threat of leaving without a forwarding address.

Ulysses is greatly moved by Billy's retelling of *The Odyssey* and is struck by the parallels with his own life. Having already aimlessly roamed the country for eight years, he comes to believe that he will be reunited with his family once ten years are up. The bond he forms with Billy also makes him rethink his insistence on always travelling alone. In return, Ulysses saves Billy from Pastor John more than once. With his inspirational tale of hiding from a twister inside a coffin, he also teaches his young friend to rely on his own resourcefulness in desperate times. Towles never clarifies whether Ulysses really is a reincarnation of the great mythical hero.

Professor Abacus Abernathe

Given his improbable name, readers question whether the author of Billy's beloved *Compendium* is who he claims to be. When Duchess suggests they go and meet him, he expects Billy to be disappointed (a little like Dorothy's anticlimactic encounter with the Wizard of Oz). However, Abernathe's office is on the fifty-fifth floor of the Empire State Building, just as he claims. He also looks like a professor in his 'wrinkled seersucker suit'.

Billy's meeting with his literary hero is a triumph of faith over cynicism. The professor is welcoming and takes delight in hearing Billy's life story. When Billy tells him about Ulysses, Abernathe shares the boy's excitement and sense of wonder, asserting that he thinks it possible that heroes can 'return' to different eras.

Abernathe's narrative reveals how an interest in heroic stories has shaped his life. Born plain Sam (the son of an insurance adjuster and a seamstress), his fascination with stories of great adventurers and explorers led him to Harvard and then New York, where he rebranded himself as Professor Abacus Abernathe.

Abacus has led a rich and interesting life. However, since the death of his wife, his world has narrowed to the confines of his office and books. His encounter with Billy and Ulysses is rejuvenating, reminding him of the vibrancy of life. After saying goodbye to Billy, he joins Ulysses on his journey, travelling across the country.

Sister Agnes

Sister Agnes is in charge of St. Nicholas's Home for Boys: the orphanage where Duchess once lived. Her calm charisma and strong moral compass remind Duchess of Emmett. The boys listen to her, not because they are made to, but because they want to.

During his stay at the orphanage, Duchess is particularly impressed by Sister Agnes's explanation of 'the Chains of Wrongdoing.' She teaches the boys that they can be free of these chains through atonement and forgiveness. Duchess, however, interprets her words literally, adopting his own system of debt and repayment when it comes to wrongdoing.

While many of the nuns expect bad behaviour from Duchess, Sister Agnes is a true Christian who sees the best in him. Overlooking the fact that Duchess breaks into the orphanage, she is pleased by the charitable way he distributes Sally's homemade preserves. When Emmett is angry at Duchess for stealing the Studebaker, she encourages him to take a more compassionate view, relating how Duchess's father abandoned him. Pointing out that Duchess's virtues have "'never had the chance to fully flourish'", she identifies Emmett as the friend who can lead him in the right direction. When Emmett points out that he already has his brother to look after, Sister Agnes reminds him that Good Samaritans help wherever they are needed.

Warden Ackerly

Ackerly is the retired former warden of Salina's work farm. A racist tyrant, he is referred to as 'Old Testament Ackerly' due to his love of brutal acts of punishment. As an authority figure, Ackerly is a direct contrast to Sister Agnes, who believes in the compassion exemplified by Jesus Christ. As part of his plan to repay old debts, Duchess pays the ex-warden a surprise visit and knocks him unconscious with an iron skillet pan. Ackerly survives, but only just.

Warden Williams

Warden Williams takes over from Ackerly at the work farm. Unlike his predecessor, he is liberal-minded and wants to rehabilitate young offenders into 'upright' citizens. However, his well-meaning inspirational talks often fall on deaf ears.

Williams recognises that Emmett is different from most of the other boys, describing his role in Jimmy Snyder's death as "'the ugly side of chance.'" When Emmett is released, the warden tries to encourage Emmett to shake off his lasting feelings of guilt. He suggests that the justice system exists to serve victims and their families but also to allow perpetrators to atone and begin afresh.

Townhouse

Emmett's former bunkmate, Townhouse, served twelve months at the Salina work farm for hiring a stolen car. As an African American, he suffered more severe punishments than the white boys under the racist Warden Ackerly. After sneaking out to the cinema with Duchess, he was given eight strokes from the switch in front of the other boys. Townhouse has to be coaxed by Duchess to hit him as a form of repayment for the incident. However, by the third punch, he has clearly been transported back to the work farm and how he suffered there.

Townhouse is determined to make the best of his future. Nevertheless, his options are limited. He tells Emmett that, as any job offered to him will involve wearing a uniform, he has decided to join the army.

Tommy Ladue

While Duchess landed Townhouse in hot water at the work farm, he also did him a favour in the case of Tommy Ladue. A mindless racist from Oklahoma, Tommy believed in segregation and unsuccessfully tried to ostracise Townhouse. When Duchess saw Tommy and a racist guard plant stolen cookies amongst Townhouse's belongings, he moved them to Tommy's footlocker instead. The episode shows the honourable side of Duchess.

Paco and Pico Gonzalez

The Gonzalez twins are indirectly responsible for Townhouse serving a twelve-month sentence at the work farm in Salina. From the age of fourteen, the enterprising brothers hire out cars booked in for minor repairs at their father's body shop. When sixteen-year-old Townhouse rented a Buick Skylark convertible from them for a date, he was arrested when the owner of the Buick saw him cruising the streets in it. Townhouse remained loyal to the twins, claiming that he had stolen the car. Paco and Pico repay him by transforming Emmett's Studebaker for free.

Maurice

When Duchess seeks out Townhouse in Harlem, he finds him with his cousin, Maurice. Maurice is hostile to Duchess, as he idolises Townhouse and likes to think of himself as his cousin's right-hand man. However, Duchess recognises that Maurice's combative attitude stems from feeling he cannot 'find his place in the world'. Freckly, he is paler than the other gang members but 'not 'white enough to be white.' Relating to how Maurice feels, Duchess throws him the keys to the Studebaker, declaring that the car is his. The grand gesture is later proved meaningless when Emmett reclaims the Studebaker.

Sarah Whitney

Sarah is Woolly's gentle and compassionate sister. Despite Woolly's talent for inadvertently getting into trouble, Sarah is always caring and welcoming while trying to conceal how much she worries about her brother. Wanting to protect him, she constantly fears what he might do next.

A good listener, Sarah is the only person Woolly can rely on to be accepting without subjecting him to a tirade of 'whos, whys, and whats'. However, this puts her in a difficult position with her husband as she frequently has to defend his actions. We see the toll on Sarah when Duchess finds her wandering around the house at night, unable to sleep, and with a bottle of pills in her pocket.

Confiding in Emmett about her fears for Woolly, Sarah says that her brother's troubles spring from his '"abundance"' of virtues. Childlike and innocent, Woolly is too nice for his own good. Emmett concludes that, in this case, Sarah's fatal virtue is 'forgiveness.' Later, after discovering Woolly's body, Emmett disposes of Sarah's empty pill bottle, knowing that she would blame herself for her brother's death.

"Dennis" Whitney

Dennis is married to Woolly's sister Sarah and works on Wall Street. Woolly always refers to his brother-in-law in quotation marks to reflect his pompous air of self-importance. While he provides Sarah with a high standard of living, he does not let her forget it. His office (full of photographic evidence of his achievements) contains not a single picture of his wife.

Dennis stands in the way of Woolly receiving his grandfather's money, having him declared unfit to inherit. He also does not attempt to disguise his disapproval and resentment of his brother-in-law. His presence adds to Woolly's feeling that he does not truly belong anywhere. Dennis's decision to send his brother-in-law to earn his keep at the stock exchange is the final tipping point for Woolly, prompting him to take his own life.

Kaitlin Wilcox

Woolly's other married sister, Kaitlin, lives in New Jersey. Less sympathetic to her brother's quirks, she becomes increasingly irate as strangers ask after Woolly's whereabouts. Woolly shows that he is frightened of Kaitlin when he hangs up as soon as he hears her voice on the phone.

Marceline Maupassant

When sixteen-year-old Duchess and his father lived at the Sunshine Hotel, Marceline Maupassant was a fellow resident. Unlike most of the inhabitants, Marceline was once genuinely successful. A famous European clown in the 1920s, he arrived in New York to play the Hippodrome just as the stock market crashed and the theatre closed. As a result, he ended up performing in the street and living in Room 49 of the Sunshine Hotel.

A sensitive soul, Marceline fell into depression and alcoholism. However, he always left his door ajar for Duchess and showed an interest in him. One morning, Duchess discovered Marceline hanging from the room's ceiling fan. Before the police arrived, Duchess's father stole Marceline's expensive gold pocket watch and, when suspicions were raised, planted it on his son. While Duchess does not acknowledge it, he is deeply scarred by the discovery of his friend's body and his father's betrayal.

In Marceline's most famous stage act, he pretended to be a panhandler, trying to get the attention of people who bustled past him. When his hat blew off, he would chase it around the stage and (just as a police officer was about to stand on it), snap his fingers to make everybody freeze. Marceline would skip amongst them before checking his pocket watch, retrieving his hat, and snapping his fingers to return everyone to normal. In the final moments before Duchess dies, he imagines that he is holding Marceline's gold watch and sees a frozen tableau as if through the great clown's eyes.

Tom Obermeyer

Mr Obermeyer is the banker who waits to greet Emmett when he returns home from Salina. He gives Emmett the news that the farm is now the bank's property.

Sheriff Petersen

Sheriff Petersen knows that Emmett is a law-abiding boy who ended up killing someone under unfortunate circumstances. He tries to look out for Emmett during his brief return to Morgen.

Ellie Matthiessen

Morgen's librarian, Ellie, is fond of Billy and admires his intellectual curiosity. She nurtures his love of reading and gives him his beloved *Compendium*.

Mr Packer & Mr Parker

Emmett encounters Mr Packer and Mr Parker in the dining car of a train. Both are recovering from a stag party, surrounded by the debris of a food fight. An eccentric pair, Mr Parker wears a slice of ham in the breast pocket of his tuxedo while Mr Packer's face is painted with ketchup stripes.

Mistaking him for a steward, Mr Parker asks Emmett to pass him a half-empty gin bottle from the floor. Unable to stand, he has been trying to work out how to reach it for an hour. As a reward, he places a fifty-dollar bill in Emmett's pocket.

Emmett is disgusted by the behaviour of Mr Parker and Mr Packer. He finds their idleness and misuse of wealth offensive. However, later in the novel, Emmett is reminded of Parker and Packer as he reflects on his own profligate behaviour at Woolly's sister's house. Emmett's reassessment of the pair shows he has learned to be less judgmental of others.

Morton & Mr Winslow

Emmett meets this performing duo in the Statler Building while trying to locate Harry Hewett's agent. Mr Morton is a kindly man who advises Emmett to pretend he is the son of a rodeo owner. Mr Winslow is an African Grey parrot.

The Sutter Sisters

The 'ASTOUNDING SUTTER SISTERS' head the bill of Red Hook's X-rated circus. Performing stunts on horseback, they shoot each other's clothes off until they are naked.

Ma Belle

Ma Belle has two personas. As Delilah, she performs in the circus, wearing a pink tutu and riding a child's tricycle. As Ma, she is the buxom, gruff-voiced madam of the backstage brothel. Formidable, but with a heart of gold, she is the closest Duchess has to a surrogate mother.

THEMES & IMAGERY

Debt & Repayment

The theme of debt and repayment runs throughout *The Lincoln Highway*. On a literal level, this is represented in the debts Charlie Watson runs up and fails to repay and in Duchess's ongoing tally of 'expenses' owed to Emmett. On a thematic level, the novel explores the moral debts individuals incur through life and asks whether it is possible to fully compensate for them.

Towles' original working title for *The Lincoln Highway* was *Unfinished Business,* and the phrase neatly sums up the agendas of several of the novel's characters. Firstly, there is the 'unfinished business' between Emmett and the Snyder family. While Jake Snyder is not a natural aggressor, he feels obligated to take some kind of revenge for his younger brother's death. Emmett, meanwhile, is in complete agreement, believing that his remorse and time at Salina are insufficient to atone for Jimmy Snyder's death. Eventually, Jake is goaded into hitting Emmett by his friend, and Emmett allows him to do so. The incident makes both parties feel slightly better.

Duchess, who witnesses the beating Emmett willingly takes, is struck by the equity of the arrangement. Suddenly, he thinks he understands Sister Agnes's talks on 'the Chains of Wrongdoing.' The head nun explained to the boys that the wrongs they experienced and inflicted would become burdens without 'atonement' and 'forgiveness.' While Sister Agnes's advice was a metaphor for sin and redemption, Duchess thinks of it as a balancing of accounts. Inspired by Emmett, he decides that he should also clear his 'unsettled debts' before making a fresh start.

Weighing up the wrong he has done Townhouse against the good turn he once did him, Duchess decides that three punches from his friend will balance the score between them. When repaying the debt owed to him by the sadistic former warden Ackerly, he settles on one blow to the head with an iron skillet. Duchess congratulates himself on resisting the temptation to hit Ackerly again, as this would then place him in Ackerly's debt. Readers, however, are reasonably sure this is not the type of moral justice Sister Agnes had in mind.

Duchess's warped notion of debt and repayment highlights the complexities of moral responsibility. While it would be convenient to precisely weigh how much is owed to one and how much one owes others, the reality is rarely that simple. The nature of Duchess's death at the end of the novel neatly encapsulates this point. While Emmett has no intention of killing his friend (and is oblivious to the fact that he has done so), his actions nevertheless lead to the tragedy.

Inheritance

During *The Lincoln Highway*, a number of the characters receive or are due legacies. The one hundred- and fifty-thousand-dollar trust fund Woolly should have inherited at eighteen plays a significant role in the plot. The small sum Emmett is left by his father is just enough to get him to California to start a new life. Personal belongings are also handed down from one character to another. Having inherited his uncle's officer's watch, Woolly then passes it on to Billy. Billy, in turn, gives the St. Christopher pendant he receives from Sister Agnes to Ulysses. These gifts represent the continuation of life through successive generations.

Through the legacies in the novel, Towles explores the idea of emotional inheritance. As well as material goods, the characters are shown to inherit family values, which may be either positive or negative. On his death, Charlie Watson leaves Emmett 'two legacies, one great, one small'. The small legacy is the three thousand dollars Charlie withheld from his creditors. While this is not an insignificant sum, it is a drop in the ocean compared to the 'stocks and bonds ... houses and paintings' Charlie inherited from his own father and gave up when he moved to Nebraska. The only 'remnants' of this former wealth to be found in the Watson house are a picnic basket and a collection of fine china gathering dust.

The 'great' portion of Emmett's legacy is a page torn from Ralph Waldo Emerson's essay, 'Self-Reliance.' Emerson's emphasis on hard work and authenticity in this essay explains why Charlie gave up everything to pursue his Emersonian dream. It also acts as a prompt for Emmett to follow his own path and fulfil his promise. Charlie's certainty that Emmett will make a success of his life is a spiritual blessing, in some ways more valuable than money. Emmett has mixed feelings about his legacies, unsure whether to feel 'disappointment or admiration' for his father. What he does know is that he is determined not to emulate him. In this way, Charlie's failures act as a spur, shaping the man that Emmett becomes. Rejecting his father's romanticism, Emmett grows to be practical and unsentimental – almost to a fault.

While Duchess's father is still alive, he is so deliberately elusive that he might as well be dead. The only item Duchess inherits from Harry is the case of Othello accessories his father mistakenly leaves behind in his haste to avoid his son. In terms of character, Harry passes down his theatricality, love of Shakespeare and dishonesty. Duchess also inherits the sins of his father when he is arrested for stealing Marceline's watch. While Duchess is a better person than Harry, he has been unavoidably shaped by his father's influence. The way in which he dies shows that he has been unable to shake off some of Harry's worst traits.

At first glance, Woolly would seem to be the most fortunate character when it comes to inheritance. He is from a wealthy family, sent to the most expensive boarding schools, and left a significant trust fund by his grandfather.

Unfortunately, Woolly's impressive origins prove worthless to him. His brother-in-law ensures he cannot lay his hands on his trust fund. Meanwhile, the Cadillac convertible his father left him sits in the garage, unused. Woolly's emotional inheritance is a feeling of loss for the relatives who have disappeared from his life: his grandfather and father through death and his mother and sister via marriage. In the end, Woolly also inherits the family curse. Like his father, uncle, and grandfather before him, he dies tragically young.

Storytelling

The Lincoln Highway is a homage to great literature and the power of storytelling. The novel is littered with references to books and plays, and its structure includes stories within stories. Towles explores the joy of reading and the many ways a tale can be told.

As they experience an adventure of their own, the main characters reference Alexander Dumas' novels *The Three Musketeers* and *The Count of Monte Cristo*. Pastor John quotes and misquotes resonant passages from the Bible. Charlie Watson leaves an inspirational page from Ralph Waldo Emerson's *Essays* as a legacy to his son. Duchess, meanwhile, introduces the rich language of Shakespeare's plays into the novel, learned from his thespian father. He also throws in obscure literary anecdotes. Duchess's claims about the unlucky history of *Macbeth*, for example, are based on fact.

Towles is also interested in exploring the many different forms a story can take. Duchess, for example, is secretly illiterate but also a compelling storyteller. He is adept at telling tall tales, as well as quoting Shakespeare from memory. Through Duchess's character, the novel pays tribute to the oral storytelling tradition. He is a reminder that narratives do not necessarily have to be told and consumed via the written word. Woolly also considers the competing merits of different literary forms. His sister's bedtime readings from the original, one-thousand-page version of *The Count of Monte*

Cristo were perfect for lulling him to sleep as a child. However, Woolly finds Professor Abernathe's concise retelling of the novel more exciting as he does not have to wait for the highlights.

Billy takes his favourite book everywhere and has read it more than twenty times. *Professor Abacus Abernathe's Compendium of Heroes, Adventurers, and Other Intrepid Travelers* plays a key role in the novel. Including the story of one adventurer for every letter of the alphabet, *The Compendium* mixes stories of mythical heroes like Achilles and Sinbad with actual historical figures such as Galileo, Napoleon, and Abraham Lincoln. Emmett is baffled by Abernathe's selection, feeling that there should be a clear line 'between fact and fancy.' However, Billy's literal-minded brother is missing the point. As far as Towles is concerned, good stories are a magical mix of fact and fantasy, just like *The Lincoln Highway* itself. This blurring of fiction and 'real life' is emphasised through the character of Ulysses, who could have stepped straight out of Billy's *Compendium.*

Through Billy, Towles reflects on the structural issues that all writers battle with. Billy delays completing the Compendium's blank chapter, titled 'You', as he wants to begin his story '*in medias res*', just as Homer did in the story of Achilles. However, his problem is in identifying the middle point of his life's adventure. In the end, Billy decides to start his story with Emmett's return from Salina: the exact point where Towles begins his meticulously structured novel.

The Lincoln Highway celebrates the power of literature, but Towles also includes a warning to fellow bibliophiles. On hearing Billy's story, Professor Abernathe is reminded of the vibrancy of life itself. Having lived exclusively through books for many years, he declares "'How easily we forget—we in the business of storytelling—that life was the point all along.'"

Mythical Journeys

The novel's relationship to classical myths is connected to the theme of storytelling. Just like Homer's story of Ulysses, *The Lincoln Highway* can be read as an odyssey, albeit set in 1950s America.

The most obvious parallel with ancient myth is in the character of Ulysses. Like the Greek hero of the same name, the African American man wants to be reunited with his wife and son after fighting overseas. His journey across America, on foot and by train, mirrors the long voyage of Ulysses across the Trojan Sea. On the way, both heroes survive trials of extreme weather. While winds blow the Greek Ulysses' ship off course, Towles' version escapes a tornado by jumping in a coffin. Both must also battle and triumph over beings who mean them harm (in *The Lincoln Highway,* this role is taken by Pastor John). Emmett, similarly, has his own odyssey to complete. On the way to California, he is blown off course to New York, largely by the force of nature that is Duchess.

Discussing myth in his *Compendium*, Professor Abernathe explains the role of the fatal flaw in preventing heroes from reaching their goals. Billy realises that his brother's fatal flaw (like that of Achilles) is anger. Emmett rarely loses his temper, but it leads to 'irreversible consequences' when he does. Having already paid the price for this flaw at Salina, Emmett battles with his temper throughout his journey. When Billy sees Emmett tussling with Duchess near the novel's end, he knows that his brother is in danger of letting his anger get the better of him. At this point, Billy decides that now is the time to play his essential role as *Xenos*. Another concept of Greek myth, *Xenos* refers to a character who intervenes 'at just the right time' to help the hero. Towles also explores the paradoxical idea that a character's virtues may hamper their progress and prove to be their fatal flaw. Woolly's sister Sarah suggests that the root of her brother's troubles is his 'abundance' of innocence. Her fears that this will lead to his doom prove to be well-founded.

Like all great myths, *The Lincoln Highway* explores the tension between free will and fate. While heroes pursue their goals with determination and perseverance, fate often catches up with them, no matter how hard they try to avoid it. Oedipus, for example, goes to great lengths to avoid fulfilling the prophecy that he will kill his father and marry his mother. Ironically, however, the cautionary steps he takes only bring him closer to this inevitable fate. Similarly, after killing Jimmy Snyder, Emmett is determined never to make the same mistake again. However, just as he is about to begin his fresh start, he accidentally causes Duchess's death. Although Emmett is oblivious to this turn of events, readers are left with the sense that he is fated to cause unintentional harm.

The Magic of Performance

The Lincoln Highway is brimming with colourful theatrics, from the outrageous acts at Red Hook Circus to the performers with animal sidekicks queueing at an entertainment agency. Duchess's stories are also full of Vaudeville artists, including the clown, Marceline Maupassant; 'Master of Telekinesis', Professor Heinrich Schweitzer; and the magician, Mandrake the Magnificent. As Duchess reveals, many of these acts were based on fakery and illusion. For example, Professor Schweitzer's telekinetic powers relied upon 'invisible wires, electricity, and jets of air.' Including these performers in the novel brings a surreal air to proceedings, blurring fantasy and realism.

The son of a vaudeville actor, Duchess views life as a performance and often uses show business analogies. For example, he compares his ride in the trunk of the warden's car to the act of escape artist Kazantikis which involved being locked inside a chest at the bottom of a tankful of water. Fittingly, when he first appears at the Watsons' farm, his first words are "'—Ta-da!'"

Viewing life as a vaudeville performance gives Duchess a

light-hearted perspective, even when things are not going his way. For example, when Woolly admits that he does not know the combination to the safe, Duchess sees the humour in the situation, declaring, 'Like I said: When it comes to vaudeville, it's all about the setup.' Even when he finds himself marooned in the rowboat, Duchess cannot help but appreciate the 'ingenuity' of Emmett's plan: 'It was like a setup for Kazantikis. The only thing better would have been if Emmett had tied my hands behind my back.' When Duchess bows to his imaginary audience, declaring, '*The rest is silence*', it is clear that his life's performance is at an end. Nevertheless, somewhere in the back of the reader's mind is the hope of a last-minute escape worthy of the great Kazantikis.

Underlying the many references to theatrics in the novel is the repeated countdown from ten to one (in the chapter structure, the magic trick Duchess teaches his friends, etc.). Towles' emphasis on magic and performance reminds readers that the act of creating fiction is, in itself, a kind of conjuring trick.

What it Means to be American

The Lincoln Highway is an unashamed celebration of all things American. The novel is littered with references to America's culture and history. The Fourth of July is a crucial date in Emmett's memories of his mother and the day when Billy hopes to find her again. The date of the Gettysburg Address turns out to be the key to opening the Wolcotts' safe. Billy keeps his precious silver dollar collection in a George Washington cigar tin. Meanwhile, the novel's backdrop is strewn with great American landmarks: the Empire State Building, Times Square, and the Brooklyn Bridge.

Towles portrays a nostalgia-tinted 1950s when America seemed to be at its most glorious. The novel highlights the iconic nature of entertainment at this point in American history. Frank Sinatra and Tony Bennett dominated the radio.

Although still in its early days, television offered classics like 'The Lone Ranger' and 'Sergeant Joe Friday'. This is also the era when movie stars (Marilyn Monroe, Gary Cooper, etc.) were at their most impossibly glamorous and charismatic.

Each of the novel's main characters is pursuing their version of the American Dream. Emmett has rejected his father's romantic, Emersonian dream of working his own land. Instead, he comes up with an alternative goal: to get rich by renovating and selling houses. Duchess's dream is to open an Italian restaurant just like Leonello's.

As is so often the case in books about the American dream, striving for a better future is shown to be more important than attaining it. Many of the characters' goals seem implausible, but we do not think any less of them for it. Billy's hope that he will spot his mother in the vast crowds at the Fourth of July fireworks in San Francisco seems unlikely to be fulfilled. Ulysses' faith that he will be reunited with his family after ten years is a long shot. Then there is Woolly, who, like F. Scott Fitzgerald's Jay Gatsby, wants to turn back time and return to a happier past. It is not the probability of the outcome that counts but the optimism that drives these dreams.

A large part of the mythos of the American dream is the notion of self-reliance. Emmett and Duchess both have this quality in abundance but apply it very differently. While Emmett aims to prosper from honest hard work, Duchess relies on his ability to talk, cheat, or con his way to success. Sally and Townhouse are also self-reliant characters, but their dreams are limited by gender and race, respectively. Sally longs to be an adventurer but is stuck in the role of an all-American homemaker. Townhouse, meanwhile, can aspire to any role, as long as it involves wearing a uniform. Through Sally and Townhouse, Towles shows that the American Dream is not as inclusive as it purports to be.

Friendship

Emmett, Billy, Duchess, and Woolly are all orphaned to one degree or another. The Watson brothers have lost their father and are searching for their missing mother. Duchess's mother died when he was young, leaving him with a heartless, mostly absent father. Woolly lost his beloved father to the war and feels that his mother has removed herself from his life by remarrying and moving to Palm Springs. The bond the four boys form is their substitute for family.

Billy has a talent for making new friends very quickly. After he accepts sandwiches from the kindly Mrs Simpson at a train station, Emmett feels he must lecture his brother about what constitutes a friendship. After much negotiation, the brothers agree on three days as the minimum time needed to get acquainted with someone before they can be considered a friend. However, Towles makes it clear that true friendship cannot be held to such constraints. While Ulysses ensures that he spends three days with Billy to meet the friend criteria, the strong connection they share is forged almost immediately.

Time

Time is important to every one of the main characters in *The Lincoln Highway*. All four of the boys have missions with tight timescales. Emmett and Billy must get to San Francisco by the Fourth of July to have any chance of finding their mother. Meanwhile, Duchess and Woolly need to retrieve one hundred and fifty thousand dollars from the house in the Adirondacks before it is opened for the summer at the end of June. Emmett, in particular, is constantly aware of time ticking away. This sense of urgency is reflected in the novel's chapter structure, which counts down from ten to one.

The passing of time is also a reminder of human mortality. Professor Abernathe becomes acutely aware of how little time he has left. Perceiving life's trajectory as 'the shape of a diamond on its side', he realises that he is swiftly heading to the final 'narrow' and 'inexorable point' that means death. With the spectre of his mortality in sight, he determines to make the most of what time he has remaining to him.

Towles highlights his theme with repeated references to timepieces. Two grandfather clocks feature in the novel: the unwound one in Sarah's house and the handless one in the train dining car. As both clocks are effectively useless, they seem to represent wasted time. Sarah lives a lonely existence as Dennis's wife. Her unwound clock (inherited from Grandfather Wolcott) also reflects Woolly's inability to turn back time to when they were a happy family. On the train, Mr Parker and Mr Packer squander their time (and money) in an inebriated haze (symbolised by the olive in a cocktail glass speared by one of the missing clock hands).

Watches also play a significant role in the novel. Billy's army surplus watch is part of his explorer's kit. Emmett borrows it during their train journey to keep an eye on the time. However, after almost falling from the train's roof, he discovers that the watch's face is smashed and the mechanism is broken. The mishap shows that, no matter how hard Emmett tries to manage time and events during his journey, both lie out of his control. Woolly eventually gives Billy a replacement watch. Owned initially by Woolly's grandfather in WWI, the officer's watch was handed down to Woolly's uncle, who died in the Spanish Civil War. When Woolly passes it on to Billy, it is a clue that he will soon be the latest deceased member of the Wolcott clan.

In Duchess's final moments, the timepiece imagery comes to a climax. Earlier in the novel, Duchess refers to Kazantikis: an escape artist who performed with a giant clock ticking down in the background. In a similar scenario, Duchess tries to escape the leaking rowboat and grab the money while counting down from ten. Unfortunately, his routine is significantly less successful than that of Kazantikis. As he drowns, he sees Marceline Maupassant's pocket watch in his hand. Here, the gold watch seems to represent the inevitability of Duchess's fate. From the moment his father framed him for its theft, his life trajectory has been set. In a poignant moment, Duchess sees his friends frozen in time, as if in Marceline's act, before the final curtain falls.

War

The 1950s was a welcome period of peace following World War II. However, the shadow of warfare lurks in the background of *The Lincoln Highway*. The Second World War had a lasting effect on Woolly, whose father died in a fighter plane. Emmett's fate is also connected to the conflict, as he hits Jimmy Snyder for implying his father was mentally unfit to enlist. Sheriff Petersen also talks about the aftermath of the war on Morgen ten years later. He observes how men who fought in the conflict returned violent, willing to pick a fight with anyone, or quietly drank themselves to death.

Towles also conveys the fear of nuclear attack that hung over America due to the Cold War. At school, Billy's class have emergency drills, preparing to hide under their desks in the event of a nuclear explosion. Meanwhile, Woolly sees newspaper photographs of an atomic bomb drill where key areas of New York were evacuated.

The Lincoln Highway

Designed in 1912 and named after Abraham Lincoln, the Lincoln Highway was the first road to stretch the length of America, from Times Square in New York City to Lincoln Park in San Francisco. When Billy finds the postcards his mother sent, he works out from the locations that she took this route when she left them, ending up in San Francisco. So begins the Watson brothers' road trip.

The great irony of Towles' novel is that Emmett and Billy never get to follow their planned course on the titular highway. Starting at a midpoint on the route, they intend to head for California, but unforeseen circumstances divert them in the opposite direction to New York.

The boys' inability to reach their intended destination is a metaphor for life. As a wise panhandler says to Emmett, "'Well, that's life in a nutshell, ain't it. Lovin' to go to one place and havin' to go to another.'" A crucial part of Emmett's psychological journey is to learn to be less rigid and adapt to the unexpected circumstances that life throws at us all. At the end of the novel, we see the Watson brothers about to begin their true journey across the Lincoln Highway. This time, they are paying full tribute to the route by starting in Times Square and travelling its entire length.

Abraham Lincoln

The name of Abraham Lincoln pops up frequently in the novel. As well as the highway named after him, he is listed as a hero in Billy's *Compendium* and his image often appears in the shape of statues or busts. Woolly's great-grandfather was a great admirer of the sixteenth American president and kept a likeness of him on his desk. Following in his footsteps, Woolly is excited to learn that there are statues of Lincoln along the highway. When Woolly goes missing, Duchess knows he will find his friend at the closest Abraham Lincoln statue in Liberty Park. In a novel that celebrates America, Lincoln is particularly significant as he is the president who reunited the country following the Civil War.

The Studebaker

Emmett's 1948 powder-blue Studebaker Land Cruiser symbolises independence. Emmett bought the vehicle with the money he earned as a carpenter. At Salina, he keeps a picture of a similar car on the wall as a reminder the Studebaker is waiting for him. When the family farm is repossessed, it is the one item the bank does not have the power to take away.

The Studebaker represents freedom and independence for

two reasons. Firstly, it is where Charlie Watson hides what little money he has left for Emmett. Secondly, it provides the means for Emmett and Billy to travel to California and make a fresh start. However, this plan is jeopardised when Duchess uses the Studebaker to travel to Ackerly's house, where he attacks the former warden. Once the police start looking for the vehicle, Emmett is incriminated in the offence, and he is forced to let the Gonzalez twins work their magic on it. To Emmett's consternation, it emerges from the paint shop a dazzling yellow. This could be Towles' ironic nod to Jay Gatsby's showy yellow car in *The Great Gatsby*.

Maps

Whether the characters can or cannot map read tells us a lot about them. Billy, for example, is a born map reader, reflecting his rationality and logic. On the other hand, neither Duchess nor Woolly can read a map, although this turns out to be for different reasons. Duchess simply cannot read but is too embarrassed to admit it. Meanwhile, Woolly dislikes ordinary road maps because they confuse his creative, child-like brain. He prefers the 'simplified map' on the Howard Johnson's placemats. Like a pirate's treasure map, complete with illustrations, it successfully shows him the way to the Abraham Lincoln statue in Liberty Park.

For Emmett, maps seem to offer a straightforward route to a new life in California. He believes he will get to his destination if he follows the right roads. However, he has not anticipated the influence of Zeno's paradox: the concept that motion is an illusion. In school, Emmett dismisses Zeno's paradox as nonsense. After travelling fifteen hundred miles in the wrong direction and ending up in New York, he is forced to reassess this opinion.

Desks

Desks symbolise masculine authority in the novel, and how

their owners use them tells us a good deal about their characters. Woolly observes that in his experience, 'people sitting behind desks' often ask to speak to you urgently and then 'sit there for a good long minute without saying a word.' Here, Woolly encapsulates the unequal power balance desks can create, whether they belong to headteachers or his brother-in-law.

Dennis's office loudly declares his sense of self-importance. Sitting behind his desk, he lectures Woolly about his bad behaviour, making him feel inadequate. No one else is allowed to sit there, as this would involve usurping Dennis's power. For this reason, Woolly knows he is in deep trouble when Dennis comes across the telephone receiver stuffed in his desk drawer (where Woolly left it earlier). His fate is confirmed when Dennis announces (from behind his desk) that he has arranged for Woolly to work on the stock exchange: a role he is patently unsuited to. This announcement prompts Woolly's suicide, and, significantly, he writes his farewell note at the desk of his great-grandfather (a man who wore his authority much more lightly than Dennis).

The portrayal of Professor Abernathe at his desk serves as a direct contrast to Dennis's high-handed authority. Confronted with unexpected guests in the form of Billy, Woolly and Duchess, we might expect the professor to use his desk as a barrier and maintain an aloof distance. Instead, he warmly welcomes them, redirecting his visitors to comfortable seats and speaking to them as equals.

Rifling through Mr Watson's desk, Duchess learns something interesting about its former owner. The drawer full of unpaid bills reflects Charlie Watson's bad decision-making and financial incompetence. In this sense, the desk represents the reverse of masculine success. However, the drawer's contents also suggest the underlying decency of the desk's owner. Duchess notes that, while his father would have thrown the bills away, Charlie Watson kept them, hoping he could someday pay his debts.

It is also no accident that we see Sally sitting at her father's desk in his absence. While Ed Ransom may like to think he is head of the household, Sally shows herself to be very much in charge. She uses his phone to locate Emmett: a task her father would certainly disapprove of.

Boats & Rivers

For a novel that has nothing to do with seafaring, *The Lincoln Highway* includes a surprising number of references to boats and water. Emmett, for example, observes that 'The Anchor' is a strange name for a seedy bar in Hell's Kitchen. He also encounters a painting of a schooner at sea when locked in a room with Charity.

The sailing imagery in the novel echoes the story of Ulysses, whose ten-year adventure took place by sea. It is a reminder that Emmett has embarked on his own epic voyage, albeit by road. Towles also uses the imagery to reflect his characters' states of mind. For example, when Emmett first enters the room with Charity, the painted ship appears to be 'in full sail'. As he leaves the next morning, however, he realises the schooner is shipwrecked, and one of the sailors is 'on the verge of being either dashed upon the rocks or swept out to sea.' The image sums up Emmett's assessment of his position, as he has once again been disastrously delayed in his quest.

Rivers and boats play a critical role in Duchess's fate, as water is shown to be his nemesis. His inability to swim leads to Townhouse being punished when they attempt a trip to the cinema from Salina. Duchess also makes himself appear foolish when he dismisses Billy and Woolly's claim that George Washington crossed the Delaware River "'standing in the bow of a rowboat'". Duchess's assertion that "'Nobody stands in the bow of a rowboat'" comes back to haunt him when he finds himself doing just that in an attempt to save his money from blowing away in the wind.

The Mysterious #8

Eight seems to be a significant number in *The Lincoln Highway*, appearing numerous times:

- Billy is eight years old
- Mrs Watson abandoned her family eight years earlier
- Duchess was eight when his father left him at the orphanage
- Emmett was eight when his family first travelled to the Seward Fourth of July fireworks
- Townhouse received eight strokes of the switch for his illicit trip to the cinema
- Emmett finally arrives at eight o'clock for dinner at Sarah's house
- Professor Abernathe reduces the plot of *The Count of Monte Cristo* to eight succinct pages
- On the count of eight, Duchess loses his balance in the boat and drowns

Surely no coincidence? The recurrence of the age of eight suggests that this is a particularly impressionable stage of a child's life. Duchess and Emmett, for example, were old enough to remember the distressing behaviour of their parents but too young to begin to understand adult motivations. For Billy, however, who is mature for his years, eight is the age when his adventures begin. The circularity of the figure eight (with no beginning or end) also reflects the trajectory of Emmett's journey, which involves constantly circling back on himself.

DISCUSSION QUESTIONS

1) *The Lincoln Highway* employs a cast of colourful and diverse characters. Who was your favourite character, and why?

2) Emmett is the protagonist of the novel, but it could be argued that Duchess is more engaging. Whose narrative did you find most compelling? Do you prefer protagonists to be morally upright or somewhat flawed?

3) Amor Towles originally intended to write *The Lincoln Highway* from the point of view of Emmett and Duchess. However, as he worked on the novel, he decided that other characters needed to be heard (Billy, Woolly, Sally, Ulysses, Pastor John, and Abacus). Did Towles make the right decision? What do the multiple perspectives add to the novel?

4) Only two narratives are told from a first-person perspective: those of Duchess and Sally. Why do you think Towles wrote their accounts in the first person? How does it affect the reader's response to them?

5) The chapters are numbered in reverse order, beginning with Ten and ending with One. Why does Towles choose to structure the novel in this way? How is this countdown effect echoed in other parts of the story?

6) Duchess is a complicated character, capable of genuine kindness and extreme callousness. Which of his actions most surprised you and why?

7) Despite being only eight years old, Billy profoundly influences several of the other characters. Why is this? Who does he affect, and how?

8) Emmett, Duchess, Woolly, and Sally are all on the brink of adulthood. How do you think they compare to young adults today?

9) *The Lincoln Highway* is, among other things, a coming-of-age novel. How do the main characters change in the course of the story? What do they learn?

10) Why do you think Emmett and Billy's mother abandoned them? Did you share Billy's belief that they would be reunited with her?

11) Inheritance is a central theme in the novel. Some of the characters receive legacies, but Towles also explores the idea of emotional inheritance. How far are Emmett and Duchess shaped by the traits and actions of their parents?

12) In his tale of the twister and the coffin, Ulysses teaches Billy the importance of trusting in one's own resources. How does Billy put this advice into action? Have you experienced a moment when you surprised yourself during a crisis?

13) New York plays a major role in the novel's events. How do the responses of Emmett, Billy, Woolly, and Duchess to the city differ? What do their differing reactions tell us about their characters?

14) Emmett tells Billy he needs to know people for at least three days before considering them friends. Do the events of the novel bear out this claim? How long does it take before you think of someone as a friend?

15) Each of the novel's main characters is pursuing their own version of the American Dream. What are the goals of Emmett, Billy, Duchess and Woolly, and how realistic are they?

16) Despite the novel's title, Emmett and Billy only begin their journey on the Lincoln Highway in the book's final pages. Did you find this frustrating? Why does Towles give this somewhat misleading title to his novel?

17) Duchess develops a moral code based on the concept of debt and repayment. How does he come up with this code? What are its pros and cons?

18) Emmett objects to how Professor Abernathe's *Compendium* mixes stories of mythical heroes with real historical figures. He believes there should be a clear line 'between fact and fancy.' What do you think Towles' view is on the matter, and how is this reflected in the style of his novel?

19) *The Lincoln Highway* celebrates the power of literature, but Towles also includes a warning from Professor Abernathe about living through books too much: "'How easily we forget—we in the business of storytelling—that life was the point all along.'" Did this resonate with you? Does life sometimes feel like an annoying distraction from the important business of reading?

20) Professor Abernathe remembers visiting a shipwreck with his father at the age of seven. The experience was a defining one, igniting his interest in great explorers and leading to his career as a writer. Can you identify a moment from the past that influenced your life choices in a similar way?

21) Timepieces feature heavily in the plot of *The Lincoln Highway*. To point out just a few, there is Marceline Maupassant's gold watch, the handless grandfather clock in the train dining car, Billy's army surplus watch, and the officer's watch Woolly inherited from his uncle. Why do you think Towles employs so much time-related imagery in the novel?

22) In Sally's narrative, she takes issue with the gendered roles of adventurers in stories, pointing out that they are always about 'some man going somewhere.' Does Sally's role in the novel subvert or reinforce this masculine bias? Were you convinced that Sally has no intention of setting up home with Emmett and Billy?

23) When Duchess finds Woolly dead, he says "'The wonder is he hath endured so long'" (a quote from *King Lear*). What does Duchess mean by this? How did you feel about Woolly's death? Can you think of any scenario where Woolly could have survived and thrived?

24) The novel features many desks. How do the desks belonging to Dennis, Charlie Watson, Ed Ransom, Woolly's great-grandfather, and Professor Abernathe relate to the theme of power and authority?

25) When Duchess threatens the Watson brothers with a gun, he is unaware that the firing pin has been removed. Afterwards, he assures Emmett that he would never have shot them. Given Duchess's history, do you think this is true?

26) During Duchess's mission to settle old scores with his father, he traces Harry Hewett to the Olympic Hotel in Syracuse. However, as far as readers know, Duchess does not get the chance to go there before

he dies. Is it possible that Duchess catches up with his father but omits the encounter from his narrative? Did Harry Hewett deserve to be on the receiving end of Duchess's Old Testament style of justice?

27) Duchess's death provides a surprise twist at the end of the novel. Did you see it coming? How did you feel about it? Who is ultimately responsible?

28) Duchess never quite fulfils the potential Sister Agnes sees in him. If he had survived, do you feel he was capable of turning his life around?

29) *The Lincoln Highway* is brimming with references to magic acts and theatrics, from the outrageous acts at Red Hook Circus to Duchess's anecdotes about Vaudevillian performers. What is the effect of these references on the tone of the novel? Did you enjoy these theatrical flourishes?

30) Is there any chance that Duchess pulled off the ultimate magic trick and survived? Would you like to see a sequel to *The Lincoln Highway*?

31) The number eight takes a mysteriously prominent role in the novel. Duchess was eight when his father left him at an orphanage. Mrs Watson abandoned her family eight years earlier. Townhouse received eight strokes of the switch for his illicit trip to the cinema. Professor Abernathe reduces the plot of *The Count of Monte Cristo* to eight concise pages, and Duchess loses his balance in the rowboat on his count of eight. Any thoughts on why?

32) How would you describe the genre of *The Lincoln Highway*? Did it remind you of any other books you have read?

33) Towles' novel is an unashamed celebration of all things American. Does it capture your own idea of America and what it means to be an American?

34) *The Lincoln Highway* is quite different in its subject matter from Towles' earlier novels, *A Gentleman in Moscow* and *Rules of Civility*. Have you read the author's earlier works? If so, did you spot any similarities or connections to his latest novel?

QUIZ QUESTIONS

1) How does Emmett plan to become rich in California?

2) Why is Billy so sure that his mother is in San Francisco?

3) What are the two legacies Charlie Watson leaves for Emmett?

4) What is the name of Sally's old pickup truck?

5) Duchess tells Billy his name comes from being born in Duchess County. How did he really get the name?

6) What stops Woolly from inheriting his one-hundred-and-fifty-thousand-dollar trust fund when he is eighteen?

7) In Woolly's narrative, how does he convey his dislike of his brother-in-law, Dennis?

8) How did Woolly accidentally burn down the goal post at his boarding school?

9) How did Duchess end up at Salina?

10) What weapon does Duchess use to take revenge on Warden Ackerly?

11) Which orange and blue landmarks is Woolly fascinated by?

12) When Emmett encounters the tuxedo-clad Mr Parker, what does he have in his breast pocket?

13) What does Woolly come across in his sister's spice rack?

14) Why doesn't Emmett realise that it could be fatal to leave Duchess in the rowboat?

15) Which Shakespearean line does Duchess quote before he dies?

QUIZ ANSWERS

1) By renovating and reselling property

2) This is the location of the final postcard she sent to her sons

3) Three thousand dollars and a page torn from Ralph Waldo Emerson's *Essays*

4) Betty

5) It was his father's sarcastic reference to his young son's fancy clothes and long hair

6) Dennis, the trustee, declares him 'temperamentally unfit' to inherit

7) He places his name in quotation marks

8) By setting fire to his thesaurus

9) His father framed him for stealing a gold watch from Marceline Maupassant's dead body

10) A cast-iron skillet

11) Howard Johnson's motels

12) A slice of ham

13) Her pills (placed there by Duchess), which he later combines with his own 'medicine' to commit suicide

14) As there is no breeze when he puts Duchess in the boat, Emmett assumes he will be able to paddle back to shore. He is unaware that a strong wind always picks up at 5 o'clock.

15) "The rest is silence" (from *King Lear*).

FURTHER READING

Rules of Civility by Amor Towles

A Gentleman in Moscow by Amor Towles

The Adventures of Huckleberry Finn by Mark Twain

Don Quixote by Miguel de Cervantes

The Count of Monte Cristo by Alexandre Dumas

The Three Musketeers by Alexandre Dumas

The Wonderful Wizard of Oz by L Frank Baum

Alice's Adventures in Wonderland by Lewis Carroll

The Grapes of Wrath by John Steinbeck

On the Road by Jack Kerouac

The Underground Railroad by Colson Whitehead

American Dirt by Jeanine Cummins

FURTHER GUIDES IN THIS SERIES

Alias Grace (Margaret Atwood)

American Dirt (Jeanine Cummins)

Anxious People (Fredrik Backman)

Beartown (Fredrik Backman)

Before We Were Yours (Lisa Wingate)

Big Little Lies (Liane Moriarty)

The Book Thief (Markus Zusak)

Circe (Madeline Miller)

Commonwealth (Ann Patchett)

Educated (Tara Westover)

The Fault in Our Stars (John Green)

The Four Winds (Kristin Hannah)

Frankenstein (Mary Shelley)

A Gentleman in Moscow (Amor Towles)

The Girl on the Train (Paula Hawkins)

Go Set a Watchman (Harper Lee)

A God in Ruins (Kate Atkinson)

The Goldfinch (Donna Tartt)

Gone Girl (Gillian Flynn)

The Great Alone (Kristin Hannah)

The Great Gatsby (F. Scott Fitzgerald)

The Grownup (Gillian Flynn)

The Guernsey Literary and Potato Peel Pie Society (Mary Ann Shaffer & Annie Burrows)

The Handmaid's Tale (Margaret Atwood

The Heart Goes Last (Margaret Atwood)

The Husband's Secret (Liane Moriarty)

I Know Why the Caged Bird Sings (Maya Angelou)

Klara and the Sun (Kazuo Ishiguro)

The Light between Oceans (M.L. Stedman)

Lincoln in the Bardo (George Saunders)

Little Fires Everywhere (Celeste Ng)

My Brilliant Friend (Elena Ferrante)

My Name is Lucy Barton (Elizabeth Strout)

The Narrow Road to the Deep North (Richard Flanagan)

The Nickel Boys (Colson Whitehead)

Normal People (Sally Rooney)

Olive, Again (Elizabeth Strout)

The Overstory (Richard Powers)

Pachinko (Min Jin Lee)

The Paying Guests (Sarah Waters)

The Secret History (Donna Tartt)

The Storied Life of A.J. Fikry (Gabrielle Zevin)

The Sympathizer (Viet Thanh Nguyen)

The Testaments (Margaret Atwood)

The Underground Railroad (Colson Whitehead)

The Vanishing Half (Bret Bennett)

Where the Crawdads Sing (Delia Owens)

BIBLIOGRAPHY

Books

Towles, Amor. *The Lincoln Highway*. Viking, 2021

Online Articles

Bachelder, Chris. "Amor Towles's New Novel Takes You on an American Road Trip." *New York Times*, 5 October 2021, Accessed 15 March 2022

Bort, Yacovissi, Jennifer. "The Lincoln Highway: A Novel." *Washington Independent Review of Books*, 5 October 2021, Accessed 16 March 2022

Cain, Hamilton. "Amor Towles's 'The Lincoln Highway' is a long and winding road through the hopes and failures of mid-century America." *The Washington Post*, 5 October 2022, Accessed 15 March 2022

McAlpin, Heller. "With four kids in an old Studebaker, Amor Towles takes readers on a real joyride." *NPR*, 5 October 2021, Accessed 16 March 2022

Nathans-Kelly, Steve. "The Lincoln Highway." *New York Journal of Books*, October 2021, Accessed 16 March 2022

O'Grady, Carrie. "The Lincoln Highway by Amor Towles review – an all-American road trip." *The Guardian*, 17 Nov 2021, Accessed 29 March 2022

Packard, Wingate. "Amor Towles follows 2 brothers on an epic road trip in fine new novel 'The Lincoln Highway'." *Seattle Times*, 24 September 2021, Accessed 16 March 2022

Patrick, Bethanne. "How Amor Towles' quintessential American road trip novel interrogates itself." *Los Angeles Times*, 5 October 2021, Accessed 15 March 2022

Preston, Alex. "The Lincoln Highway by Amor Towles review – a love letter to the American road trip." *The Guardian*, 24 October 2021, Accessed 28 April 2022

Websites

https://www.amortowles.com/

ABOUT THE AUTHOR

Kathryn Cope graduated in English Literature from Manchester University and has a master's degree in contemporary fiction from the University of York. She is the author of Study Guides for Book Clubs and the HarperCollins Official Book Club guides. She lives in the Staffordshire Moorlands with her husband, son and dog.

Made in the USA
Columbia, SC
17 October 2022

69609527R00061